INTERNATIONAL
WHOLE MEALS

INTERNATIONAL WHOLE MEALS

Gai Stern

PRISM
PRESS

First published in Australasia in 1986 by
Nature & Health Books
This edition published in Great Britain by
Prism Press, 2 South Street, Bridport,
Dorset DT6 3NQ, England
and in the United States of America by
Prism Press, P.O. Box 778,
San Leandro, CA 94577.

ISBN 0 907061 93 1

641.5'637

Series editor: Nevill Drury
Editor: Penny Walker
Design: Craig Peterson

Typeset by Deblaere Typesetting Pty. Ltd., Sydney
Printed in Australia by The Book Printer

CONTENTS

INTRODUCTION

This book is quite a trip! A culinary journey through the cuisines of the world, *International Whole Meals* takes us from the countries of Europe and the Middle East, through Asia to the Americas.

The emphasis throughout is very much on the *wholeness* of the meals with a preference for fresh, unprocessed foods... the foods of the people, bought from the local markets and transformed – invariably by the women of the world – into delicious fare.

The recipes are pretty much authentic, although some substitutions have been made where necessary. Whole foods take over from their devitalised, processed counterparts and in most cases the flavours are more robust as a result. Food simply tastes better once its anaesthetising, addictive elements are removed. Most of the recipes which appear in this book use vegisalt, tamari or miso instead of salt; honey, maple syrup or brown sugar rather than white sugar, and, of course, brown rice and wholemeal flour win out over the inert, white varieties.

Without wanting to be fussy about food, I do believe it is possible to *enjoy* that which is also good for us. Putting wholesome food into our systems is somehow equated with a goody-two-shoes image, rather than respected. What a crazy, self-destructive world we live in! It seems clear to me that eating well comes out of feeling positive and that the better we feel about ourselves and our lives, the less likely we are to eat things that will harm us.

So, back to *International Whole Meals*. The recipes which follow are tasty, nourishing and healthy. Not *too* good for this world, but pretty close! There is very little meat content among the dishes, although the book is not exclusively vegetarian since it is concentrating on the ideal of *whole* foods. In the context of such a holistic approach, I feel animal products such as fish, chicken and eggs are a fact of the modern, Western diet. To me, they are acceptable where red meat is not. This is purely a subjective approach, although I come across many people who share this outlook. White meats and dairy products do make a valuable nutritional contribution. It should be stressed here, however, that whenever eggs or poultry are called for, it is most definitely worth seeking out the free or open-range variety. Similarly, it is infinitely preferable to eat the freshest fish you can find.

But as with all things, it's not worth giving yourself a hard time if you do eat things that are 'bad' for you. That only makes it worse. It's best to concentrate on enjoying what you eat.

By far the majority of the recipes in this book call for fresh fruit and vegetables. If you can get home-grown ones, so much the better. If not, don't forget to wash everything thoroughly if you don't want to swallow too much in the way of pesticides. If you can manage a pot of herbs or some fresh sprouts, it does help. It's certainly a positive thing to be in direct contact with the life-force that sustains us all whenever and however the opportunity arises.

So, enjoy your global epicurean adventures. Take delight in these **health-giving dishes from around the world and may the life-force be with you with every mouthful you take!**

Gai Stern

ITALY

In the days of the Roman Empire, Italians were said to have conquered the world with their cuisine and there are certainly many converts to the faith even to this day. For some modern-day devotees, however, the idea of wholemeal pasta is sacrilegious, while the use of any oil but olive oil unthinkable. Conversely, the idea of Italian food is anathema to modern day health food freaks. The following collection of recipes is an attempt to marry the two extremes so that we can all enjoy La Cucina Italiana.

Note: Soya or safflower oil can be used as a substitute for olive oil in any of the following recipes, if desired.

Antipasto

The Antipasto plate is the 'before the meal' course. It varies from region to region, season to season and may consist of one or one hundred dishes. Here are a few suggestions...

ARTICHOKES WITH LEMON *Carciofi con limone*

4 LARGE ARTICHOKES
3 TABLESPOONS OLIVE OIL
1 TEASPOON FENNEL
1 LARGE LEMON, JUICED
1 CLOVE GARLIC, CRUSHED
SALT AND PEPPER TO TASTE

Cook artichokes in boiling water until done: 35-40 minutes. Split each artichoke in half lengthways and place in glass or ceramic dish. Mix together remaining ingredients and pour over artichokes. Refrigerate at least one hour before serving.

FIGS AND PROSCIUTTO *Fichi e Prosciutto*

16 FRESH FIGS
8 THIN SLICES PROSCIUTTO (HAM)

Chill the figs. If fresh, skin them; if canned, drain them. Slice the figs lengthways and place four halves on each slice of prosciutto (canned figs can be used if fresh ones aren't available).

Other Suggestions

- Garbanzos (chick peas) cooked and marinated in oil, vinegar, garlic, basil and wine

- Pickled mushrooms, capsicum, eggplant, carrots, cauliflower. In all cases, slice the vegetables into bite-sized pieces, steam them briefly — about five minutes — and then marinate them for several hours or overnight in a dressing of olive oil, vinegar, lemon juice, dry white wine (optional), garlic, peppercorns and herbs (eg basil, thyme, bay leaves, oregano).

- Hard boiled eggs, halved and topped with soy mayonnaise

- Raw vegetables, eg carrots, celery, radishes, fennel, capsicum

- Sardines, tuna chunks, anchovies, smoked oysters

- Italian cheeses eg slices of mozzarella, provolone or gorgonzola

Egg Dishes

Use free range eggs if possible. They are vastly superior to battery eggs, both in nutritional value and flavour.

EGGS FLORENTINE *Uova alla Fiorentina*

This dish is famous for a very good reason — it is both simple and delicious!

1 BUNCH SPINACH
1 SMALL LEMON, JUICED
1 TABLESPOON OLIVE OIL
SEA SALT AND FRESHLY GROUND BLACK PEPPER TO TASTE
4 FRESH EGGS
4 TABLESPOONS FRESH PARMESAN

Wash the spinach well, separate the green parts from the stalks, then steam for 5 minutes. Leave in covered pan for a further 5 or 10 minutes until it becomes limp. Remove to a mixing bowl, chop finely, then stir in lemon juice, olive oil and seasoning. Butter four ramekins or individual ovenproof dishes and line each with the spinach mixture so that little nests are formed. Break an egg gently into each nest and top with grated parmesan. Bake for 15-20 minutes at 190°C (375°F) or until eggs are set and cheese is golden.

ROMAN EGG SOUP – *Stracciatella*

1 LITRE STOCK, CHICKEN OR VEGETABLE

4 EGGS (FREE RANGE)

2 TABLESPOONS FRESH PARMESAN CHEESE, FINELY GRATED

1 TABLESPOON TAMARI

2 TABLESPOONS WHOLEMEAL FLOUR

PINCH CAYENNE PEPPER

PARSLEY, FOR GARNISH

Slowly bring stock to the boil. Meanwhile heat eggs until thick. Add remaining ingredients to eggs and stir well, then slowly pour this mixture into the stock, stirring constantly. Continue stirring over a low light and cook a further five minutes. Garnish with parsley and serve immediately.

CLAM OMELETTE *Frittata con le Arselle*

4 EGGS (FREE RANGE)

2 TABLESPOONS PARSLEY, CHOPPED

SEA SALT AND FRESHLY GROUND BLACK PEPPER, TO TASTE

1 CAN BABY CLAMS (125 g)

1 SMALL RED PEPPER, FINELY CHOPPED

30 g BUTTER OR OLIVE OIL

Beat the eggs lightly with parsley, salt and pepper (be generous with the pepper). Add the drained clams and red pepper. Heat butter or oil in a heavy frying pan, then pour in the egg and clam mixture and cook over a low light until the underside is set. Hold a dish on top of the Frittata then turn the pan over so that it slides out. Then slide it back into the pan and brown the other side. Serve hot with a salad.

Rice Dishes

GREEN RISOTTO *Risotto Verde*

500g BROCCOLI, CHOPPED
250g ZUCCHINI, CHOPPED
30 BUTTER
1 LARGE ONION, CHOPPED
2 CLOVES GARLIC, CRUSHED
50g PINE NUTS
2 EGGS (FREE RANGE)
100g RICOTTA CHEESE
100ml MILK
1 TABLESPOON TAMARI
PINCH CAYENNE PEPPER
75g COOKED BROWN RICE
1 TABLESPOON PARMESAN CHEESE
1 TABLESPOON FRESH BASIL

Steam the broccoli and zucchini for five to ten minutes according to the size of the pieces, so that they are tender but still crunchy. Meanwhile, melt the butter and add onion and garlic. Cook for 10 minutes over a low light then add the pine nuts for a few minutes. In another bowl, beat the eggs well and then add the ricotta cheese and milk (this can be done in a blender or food processor). Season this sauce with tamari and cayenne. Mix together vegetables, rice and cheese sauce and then turn into a greased casserole dish. Top with grated parmesan and bake fo 20 minutes at 180°C (350°F). Garnish with basil leaves.

RISOTTO WITH FENNEL *Risotto con i Finocchi*

2 STALKS FLORENCE FENNEL

1 LARGE ONION, THINLY SLICED

75g BUTTER (UNSALTED IS BEST)

3 CUPS BROWN RICE

10 CUPS VEGETABLE STOCK

1 TABLESPOON TAMARI

100g FRESH PARMESAN CHEESE, GRATED

Cut the feathery tops off the fennel and put aside. Wash the bulbs and slice them thinly, then add to the onion. Heat half the butter and add the fennel and onion. Cook slowly until the vegetables start to soften, then add the rice and stir well. After a few minutes pour in half the stock (it is best if the stock is boiling) and cook over a moderate heat until the stock has been absorbed. Add the remaining stock, cover the pan and cook until the liquid is absorbed once again. The whole procedure takes about 45 minutes. When cooked, stir in tamari, the remaining butter, and parmesan cheese. Cover and leave a couple of minutes before serving. Garnish with fennel tops.

Vegetables

In Italy these are rarely eaten in their plain state. Usually they are dressed up in some exotic manner with sauces and herbs. Here are a few that can be served as an accompaniment to the main meal. Alternatively, if supplemented with just a salad, they make delicious meals in themselves.

SICILIAN CAULIFLOWER *Cavolfiore alla Siciliana*

1 kg CAULIFLOWER

200g OLIVE OIL

1 LARGE ONION, CHOPPED

15 OLIVES, PITTED AND SLICED

3 ANCHOVY FILLETS

200g CACIOCAVALLO (SMOKED) CHEESE

SEA SALT AND FRESH BLACK PEPPER

250ml RED WINE

Wash cauliflower and separate into florets. Pound anchovies. Warm 2 tablespoons of olive oil in a casserole dish, then add some of the onion, olives and anchovies. Cover with a layer of cauliflower, a few slices of the cheese, some seasoning (not too much as there are a lot of strong flavours in this dish) and a sprinkling of oil. Repeat this procedure until all the ingredients have been used up, finishing with a layer of cauliflower and oil. Pour in the wine, cover and cook for about half an hour over a moderate light, by which time the wine should have evaporated. Serve hot.

STUFFED ONIONS *Cipolle Imbottite*

| 6 LARGE ONIONS |
| 2 TABLESPOONS BUTTER |
| 3 SLICES WHOLEMEAL BREAD, GRATED TO FORM FRESH BREADCRUMBS |
| 2 TABLESPOONS OLIVE OIL |
| 1 CUP COOKED BROWN RICE |
| 1 TEASPOON OREGANO, CHOPPED |
| 2 TEASPOONS PARSLEY, CHOPPED |
| SALT AND PEPPER |
| 1 EGG, LIGHTLY BEATEN |

Peel onions and cut a fine slice from the top and bottom of each one so that they stand up in a pan. Steam the onions for 10 minutes or until they are tender but not soft. Leave to cool. Meanwhile melt butter and stir in one-third of the breadcrumbs, then set this mixture aside. Heat one tablespoon of oil. Scoop centres out of the onions with a sharp knife, chop finely and add to oil. Mix in rice, remaining breadcrumbs, herbs and seasoning, and stir well. Remove from heat and add the egg. Fill the onions with this mixture, place in a casserole dish and drizzle with remaining oil. Bake at 180°C (350°F) for one hour.

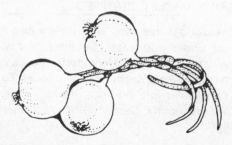

MINTED MUSHROOMS *Funghi Porcini al Tegame*

2 TABLESPOONS OLIVE OIL

1 kg MUSHROOMS, CLEANED AND SLICED

3 ANCHOVY FILLETS, CHOPPED

2 CLOVES GARLIC, CRUSHED

1 kg TOMATOES, SKINNED AND CHOPPED

3 TABLESPOONS FRESH MINT, FINELY CHOPPED

1 TABLESPOON TAMARI

PINCH CAYENNE PEPPER

Heat the oil in a heavy pan. Add mushrooms, anchovies, garlic, tomatoes, mint, tamari and cayenne. Cover and cook over a moderate heat for about 20 minutes, stirring occasionally.

Salads

PASTA SALAD *Insalata alla Fusilli*

Any spiral pasta can be used to create this salad.

150 g PASTA

100 ml OLIVE OIL

½ TEASPOON HONEY

50 ml WHITE WINE VINEGAR

SEA SALT AND PEPPER, TO TASTE

350 COLD CHICKEN, CHOPPED

50 g PINE NUTS

1 MIGNONETTE LETTUCE

1 SMALL ONION, FINELY SLICED

3 TABLESPOONS PARSLEY, CHOPPED

Cook pasta in boiling water until 'al dente' (or firm to the tooth). Drain and rinse under cold water. Combine oil, honey, vinegar, salt and pepper and whisk well. Mix together pasta, chicken, pine nuts and dressing and leave to chill for a few hours. To serve, wash lettuce and tear leaves into bite-size pieces. Add to salad with onion rings and toss gently. Garnish with a few onion rings and a sprig of parsley.

Pasta

Lasagne, vermicelli, linguine, tagliatelle, macaroni and spaghetti are just a tiny part of the Italian cuisine known collectively as pasta. You can buy it fresh from specialty stores or pre-cooked from supermarkets. Health food stores stock wholefood varieties and delicatessens carry good quality brands. You can even make it yourself. Cook it in plenty of boiling, salted water to which a tablespoon of oil has been added to prevent it from sticking. Cooking time varies according to the type of pasta but you will know it is ready when it is al dente.

EGG PASTA *Pasta Gialla*

500 g WHOLEMEAL FLOUR

4 EGGS

Put the flour in a mixing bowl or onto a pastry board and make a well in the centre. Add the lightly beaten eggs one at a time and mix well until a ball of dough is formed. Knead energetically for about 15 minutes until the dough becomes smooth and elastic, then cover and set aside for about half an hour. Roll out lightly into paper-thin, even sheets, dusting with flour as necessary. For ravioli, use immediately.

SPAGHETTI WITH WALNUTS *Spaghetti e Salsa di Noci*

250 g GROUND WALNUTS

50 g TOASTED PINE NUTS

1 CLOVE GARLIC, CRUSHED

3 TABLESPOONS FRESH BASIL, VERY FINELY CHOPPED

125 g RICOTTA CHEESE

4 TABLESPOONS OLIVE OIL

SALT AND PEPPER TO TASTE

750 g SPAGHETTI

4 TABLESPOONS BUTTER

125 g FRESH PARMESAN CHEESE, GRATED

Blend the walnuts, pine nuts, garlic and basil until smooth. Introduce the ricotta cheese and mix well, adding a tablespoon of olive oil and water, then add the remaining oil until the mixture is well blended. Add seasoning. Meanwhile, cook the spaghetti and drain. Serve at once with the sauce, butter and parmesan cheese.

GREEN PASTA *Pasta verde*

Proceed as for Egg Pasta but include a bunch of spinach that has been cooked, chopped and squeezed dry. For the lasagne recipe which follows, cut the dough into 75 mm (3") squares and leave to dry for 2 hours. When you are ready to use it, cook it in boiling, salted water for 2 minutes, then leave to drain.

PUMPKIN RAVIOLI *Tortelli di Zucca*

1 kg PUMPKIN
1 TEASPOON BLACK MUSTARD SEEDS
250 PINE NUTS
PINCH GRATED NUTMEG
SEA SALT TO TASTE
1 TEASPOON WHITE MUSTARD SEEDS
2 TABLESPOONS FRESH BREADCRUMBS
FRESHLY GROUND BLACK PEPPER
1 TABLESPOON OIL
100 g BUTTER
250 g FRESH PARMESAN CHEESE, (GRATED)

Steam pumpkin until tender, then mash until smooth. Add all remaining ingredients except parmesan and butter and mix well. Place teaspoonsful of the pumpkin mixture onto the pasta sheets at 50 mm (2") intervals. Cover with a second sheet of pasta and press down firmly between the mounds. Cut with a pastry wheel or sharp knife, making sure the edges are firmly sealed. Leave the ravioli to dry on a floured board for half an hour, turning once.
Bring a large pan of salted water to the boil. Add a tablespoon of oil and then add the ravioli, a few at a time to prevent them from sticking to each other, and cook quickly for 10 minutes or until they are soft and have risen to the top of the pot. Remove with a slotted spoon and keep warm. When all the ravioli are cooked, serve them immediately, topped with butter and parmesan cheese.

COUNTRY LASAGNE *Lasagne Rustica*

Just as good in the city!

1 kg RICOTTA CHEESE

250 g FRESH PARMESAN CHEESE, GRATED

3 EGGS, LIGHTLY BEATEN

3 TABLESPOONS PARSLEY, CHOPPED

SALT, PEPPER AND NUTMEG, TO TASTE

1 LITRE TOMATO SAUCE (SEE FOLLOWING RECIPE)

1 PACKET LASAGNE

750 g MOZZARELLA CHEESE, COARSELY GRATED

Mix together ricotta cheese, parmesan, eggs, parsley and seasonings. Now, butter a baking dish and spread some tomato sauce on
the bottom. Cover with a layer of lasagne, then layers of the
ricotta filling, tomato sauce and mozzarella. Repeat until all the
ingredients have been used up, making sure you end up with
tomato sauce. Cover and bake at 190°C (375°F) for 40 minutes,
then uncover and bake for a further 10 minutes. Let stand 5-10
minutes before serving. The lasagne is very good with garlic bread
and a crisp green salad.

TOMATO SAUCE *Sugo*

This is a simple sugo — more complex varieties call for the addition
of mushrooms, capsicums and other vegetables. Experiment until
you find the combination of ingredients you prefer.

2 TABLESPOONS OLIVE OIL

1 ONION, CHOPPED

2 CLOVES GARLIC, CRUSHED

500 g TOMATOES, SKINNED AND CHOPPED

PINCH OREGANO AND BASIL

1 GLASS DRY RED WINE

1 TABLESPOON PARSLEY, CHOPPED

SALT AND PEPPER, TO TASTE

Heat oil, and cook onions and garlic gently until soft. Add remaining ingredients, cover and simmer for at least three-quarters of an
hour. Stir the sauce occasionally, adding a little water if it cooks
down too much.

Desserts

Most Italian desserts are very sweet – hence the expression
La Dolce Vita! The sugarless ones that appear below are not
strictly authentic, but they are still pretty good...

RICOTTA PIE *Torta di Ricotta*

Pastry

1 CUP BUTTER

2 CUPS WHOLEMEAL FLOUR

2 EGG YOLKS, LIGHTLY BEATEN

1-2 TABLESPOONS COLD WATER

Cut butter into flour then mix with fingertips until it resembles
breadcrumbs. Gradually stir in egg yolks and enough water to
hold dough together. Place in buttered and floured 25cm (9")
cake tin and refrigerate until required.

Filling

750g RICOTTA CHEESE

3 TABLESPOONS FLOUR

2 TABLESPOONS ORANGE PEEL, FINELY GRATED

2 TABLESPOONS LEMON PEEL, FINELY GRATED

1 TABLESPOON VANILLA EXTRACT

4 FRESH EGGS

100ml MAPLE SYRUP

2 TABLESPOONS TOASTED COCONUT

Combine ricotta, flour, peels and vanilla. Beat eggs until frothy
then add maple syrup. Add sweetened eggs to ricotta mixture
and pour into pastry case. Bake at 180°C (350°F) for 55-60
minutes or until the ricotta mixture has set and the pastry is gol-
den brown. Remove and place on a wire rack to cool. To serve,
sprinkle with toasted coconut and cut into wedges.

HONEYED CHESTNUTS *Busecchina*

500g DRIED CHESTNUTS

250ml DRY WHITE WINE

2 TABLESPOONS HONEY

250ml CREAM

Soak the chestnuts overnight in the wine. If the liquid does not cover the chestnuts, add water. Next day, cook the chestnuts in the liquid over a low flame for 15 minutes, then add the honey, stirring well. Cook for a further 10 minutes until the chestnuts are tender and most of the liquid has been absorbed. Chill and serve with cream.

CHEESE AND FRUIT *Formaggio e Frutta*

Here are a few good combinations:

- *Bel Paese* – a creamy cheese of the North – with cherries or plums

- *Gorgonzola* – Italian blue (or green) vein cheese – with apples, pears or bananas

- *Provolone* – a bland Southern cheese similar to Mozzarella – with quartered apples or slices of canteloupe or watermelon

- *Ricotta* – a mild, pot cheese – perfect with many fruits, and excellent with berries or figs.

FRANCE

Although it is, without a doubt, the finest in the world, French food is notoriously rich. However, these days – thanks to 'La Nouvelle Cuisine' – the modern trend in French cooking is for light, but equally delicious fare.

The extensive use of dairy foods and heavy red meats swimming in thick sauces has given way to poached fish and lightly steamed vegetables floating on glistening beds of subtle 'coulis' or purées, followed by simple fruit desserts.

Despite 'La Nouvelle Cuisine', nothing beats a buttery Parisian croissant or a crusty French baguette, but these delights – fortunately, from the point of view of one's health – are not to be had in Australia. Instead, we can have the best of the new Cuisine Santé – healthy, appetising food that melts in the mouth and brings joy to the heart without overworking the liver or distressing one's vital organs.

The recipes which follow are essentially French, simple to prepare and irresistible to eat. Bon appetit!

CHICKEN STOCK – *Fond de Volaille*

Here is a simple recipe for a chicken stock which can be used in a great variety of dishes.

1 kg CHICKEN BONES AND GIBLETS

2 LITRES WATER

125 ml DRY WHITE WINE

250 g MIXED CHOPPED VEGETABLES, INCLUDING ONION, LEEK, SHALLOT, CARROT AND CELERY

2 CLOVES GARLIC, CRUSHED

1 BOUQUET GARNI

PINCH VEGISALT

Place all ingredients in a large pot. Bring to the boil then reduce to simmer gently for 2-3 hours. You will have to skim the froth off the top of the stock from time to time during the cooking process. Strain stock, cool and refrigerate to use as required.

N.B. For a vegetarian stock, omit the chicken and substitute with vegetables, including onion skins, celery leaves, carrot tops and so forth. When using vegetable stock, it is a good idea to add a spoonful or two of miso to soups just before serving.

GREEN LEEK AND POTATO SOUP – *Vichyssoise Verte*

750 ml CHICKEN OR VEGETABLE STOCK

2 MEDIUM SIZED POTATOES, DICED

1-2 LEEKS, THOROUGHLY WASHED AND FINELY CHOPPED

250 g PEAS, FRESH OR FROZEN

VEGISALT AND FRESHLY GROUND BLACK PEPPER

250 ml CREAM

2 TABLESPOONS CHIVES, FINELY CHOPPED

Bring stock to boil then add potatoes and leeks. Reduce to simmer 10-15 minutes or until vegetables are tender. Add peas and simmer for a further 5-10 minutes. Liquidise the soup in a blender or food processor then allow to cool. Season to taste with vegisalt and pepper, then stir in cream. Chill thoroughly and serve garnished with chives.

FRENCH ONION SOUP – *Soupe à l'Oignon*

This warming, delicious broth is the essence of French cuisine, showing how a masterpiece can be created from the most basic of ingredients.

2 TABLESPOONS OLIVE OIL

4-5 MEDIUM SIZED ONIONS, FINELY SLICED

PINCH BROWN SUGAR

1 LITRE CHICKEN OR VEGETABLE STOCK

VEGISALT AND FRESHLY GROUND BLACK PEPPER

3 TABLESPOONS BRANDY (OPTIONAL)

4 SLICES CRUSTY BREAD

GRATED GRUYÈRE CHEESE

Heat oil then sauté onions and sugar over a very low light until soft. The pot should be covered and the process takes about 20 minutes. When the onions are cooked, gradually add stock, bring to the boil, then reduce to simmer for 15-20 minutes. Before serving, add vegisalt, black pepper and brandy. Ladle soup into individual ovenproof dishes. Top each dish with a slice of bread and plenty of grated cheese and either place under a griller or bake in a moderate oven until the top is golden brown and crusty.

STUFFED CELERY – *Céleris Farcis*

2 STALKS CELERY, WASHED AND DRIED

2 TABLESPOONS RICOTTA CHEESE

1 TEASPOON MILK

4-5 BLACK OLIVES, PITTED AND FINELY CHOPPED

PINCH VEGISALT

PINCH CAYENNE PEPPER

PAPRIKA TO GARNISH

Trim celery and set aside. Mix together all remaining ingredients except paprika. Use this mixture to fill celery stalks which should then be cut into bite sized pieces. Sprinkle with paprika and serve.

WHITE BEAN PATÉ – *Pâté des Haricots*

1 TABLESPOON GOOD QUALITY OIL

PINCH CAYENNE PEPPER

1 TEASPOON TAMARI OR SOYA SAUCE

1 TABLESPOON MELTED BUTTER

1 CLOVE GARLIC, CRUSHED

2 CUPS COOKED HARICOT BEANS

2 TABLESPOONS SHERRY

2 TABLESPOONS PARSLEY, CHOPPED

Heat oil and sauté garlic for 5 minutes. Add cayenne and beans and cook until mixture is very soft, stirring all the time. Add tamari and sherry and cook a couple of minutes, then pile mixture into a buttered crock. Pour melted butter over top, sprinkle with parsley and chill.

GREEK VEGETABLES, FRENCH STYLE – *Legumes à la Greque*

500g MIXED VEGETABLES, CHOPPED INTO BITE SIZED PIECES – ARTICHOKE HEARTS, GREEN BEANS, LEEKS, SHALLOTS, RADISHES, CELERY, CARROT, ZUCCHINI, MUSHROOMS, CAPSICUM AND EGGPLANT ARE ALL SUITABLE

2 TABLESPOONS OLIVE OIL

2 TABLESPOONS LEMON JUICE

3-4 TABLESPOONS WATER

1 BAY LEAF

A FEW PEPPERCORNS – GREEN OR BLACK

PINCH VEGISALT

3 TOMATOES, SKINNED AND CHOPPED

Place all ingredients in a pan and bring to the boil. Reduce to simmer, uncovered, for 20 minutes or until all vegetables are cooked. Allow to cool and serve at room temperature.

ONION TARTE – *Tarte aux Oignons*

6 MEDIUM SIZED ONIONS, FINELY SLICED
PINCH CAYENNE PEPPER
3 EGGS, LIGHTLY BEATEN
1 PIE CRUST
PINCH VEGISALT
3 RASHERS BACON, DICED
3 TABLESPOONS CREAM
3 TABLESPOONS MELTED BUTTER

Blanch onions and vegisalt in boiling water. Drain and then sauté with bacon and cayenne until golden brown. Place onion mixture in pie crust and allow to cool. Meanwhile beat eggs and cream then pour over onions. Drizzle with melted butter and bake in a hot (400°F/200°C) oven for 30 minutes or until golden brown. Serve hot with a green salad.

SCALLOPS IN WHITE WINE –
Coquilles Saint Jacques au Vin Blanc

125 ml WHITE WINE
6 SCALLOPS, CLEANED
2 ONIONS FINELY CHOPPED
1 CLOVE GARLIC, CRUSHED
PINCH VEGISALT
FRESHLY GROUND BLACK PEPPER
2 TABLESPOONS BREADCRUMBS
2 TABLESPOONS PARSLEY, CHOPPED

Pour wine into a shallow baking dish. Add scallops and cover with onions and garlic. Sprinkle with salt and pepper to taste and top with breadcrumbs. Bake in a hot (400°F/200°C) oven for 10-15 minutes. Garnish with chopped parsley and serve immediately.

CRAB AND GRAPEFRUIT SALAD –
Salade de Crabe au Pamplemousse

500g FRESH CRAB MEAT

12 ASPARAGUS STALKS

1 GRAPEFRUIT

1 TABLESPOON LEMON JUICE

1 TEASPOON TOMATO PASTE

PINCH CAYENNE PEPPER

1 TEASPOON FRESH TARRAGON, FINELY CHOPPED

A FEW LETTUCE LEAVES – MIGNONETTE ARE BEST

1 TABLESPOON PARSLEY, FINELY CHOPPED

250g GREEN BEANS

125g MUNG BEAN SPROUTS

2 TABLESPOONS WALNUT OIL

1 TABLESPOON SOYA MAYONNAISE

½ TEASPOON MUSTARD

PINCH VEGISALT

Cut green beans and asparagus into 5cm (2 inch) lengths and drop into rapidly boiling salted water for about 5 minutes or until tender but still crunchy. Drain and refresh with cold water. Mix together crab meat, green beans, asparagus stalks and mung beans sprouts and set aside. Peel grapefruit, remove all pith and then dice the flesh. Combine walnut oil, lemon juice, soya mayonnaise, tomato paste, mustard, cayenne, vegisalt and tarragon in a glass jar. Screw the lid on tightly and shake well. Pour this dressing over the crab mixture. Pile the dressed crab on the lettuce leaves and garnish with grapefruit and parsley.

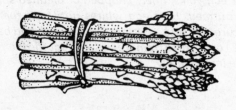

OYSTERS IN CHAMPAGNE – *Huîtres au Champagne*

These look spectacular if served on their shells and arranged on a platter of salt crystals. If this is not possible, serve them in individual dishes.

12 OYSTERS
2 EGG YOLKS
1 TEASPOON WATER
PARSLEY SPRIGS TO GARNISH
8 TABLESPOONS CHAMPAGNE
1 TEASPOON CREAM
PINCH CAYENNE PEPPER

Poach oysters in their own juice or a little water for one minute. Place champagne in a pan and bring to the boil. Continue to boil until the champagne reduces significantly, then allow it to cool. Stir in beaten egg yolks, cream and water. Place on top of a double boiler and whisk vigorously until the mixture thickens like a custard. Season with cayenne and remove from heat. Whisk again so that the sauce is frothy and then pour over the oysters. Place the oysters under a hot griller or in a hot oven for a minute or so until they become golden. Garnish with parsley and serve immediately.

SPINACH SOUFFLÉ – *Soufflé aux Epinards*

2 EGGS, SEPARATED
2 CUPS SPINACH, COOKED
VEGISALT, TO TASTE
FRESHLY GROUND BLACK PEPPER
PINCH NUTMEG

Mix together egg yolks, finely chopped or blended spinach, salt, pepper and nutmeg. Beat egg whites until stiff then fold into spinach mixture. Pile into a buttered soufflé dish and bake in a hot (375°F/190°C) oven for 20 minutes or until soufflé has risen and is golden. Serve immediately.

CELERY WITH PEPPER – *Céleris au Poivre*

3 STICKS CELERY, CUT INTO JULIENNE (MATCHSTICK) STRIPS

2 TOMATOES, SKINNED AND CHOPPED

PINCH VEGISALT

3 PEPPERCORNS, CRUSHED WITH THE BLADE OF A KNIFE

Place all ingredients in a pot and simmer gently for 20 minutes or until the celery is tender. Serve hot or cold.

FLEMISH CHICORY – *Endives à la Flamande*

6 HEADS BELGIAN CHICORY OR CHICONS

2 TABLESPOONS BUTTER

2 TEASPOONS TAMARI OR SOYA SAUCE

Clean chicory and slice into 1 cm (4 inch) rounds. Pile onto a buttered casserole dish, sprinkling the layers with tamari as you go. Top with butter and cover tightly. Bake in a warm (300°F/150°C) oven for 2 hours. To serve, turn the chicory upside down.

BEANS NIÇOISE – *Haricots Verts à la Niçoise*

250 g GREEN BEANS, TOPPED AND TAILED AND STRINGED IF TOUGH, OR LEFT WHOLE IF YOUNG AND TENDER

3 TOMATOES, SKINNED AND CHOPPED

2 CLOVES GARLIC, CRUSHED

SALT AND PEPPER, TO TASTE

1 TABLESPOON CHOPPED PARSLEY

PINCH CUMIN

Steam beans until tender but still crunchy. Place tomatoes in a pot with the garlic, salt, pepper and cumin and cook gently for 5 minutes. Add beans and heat through. Serve hot garnished with parsley.

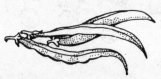

LEEKS WITH MINT – *Poireaux à la Menthe*

12 LEEKS, WHITE PARTS ONLY

2 TABLESPOONS FRESH MINT, FINELY CHOPPED

3 TABLESPOONS CHICKEN OR VEGETABLE STOCK

½ TEASPOON LEMON JUICE

PINCH VEGISALT

FRESHLY GROUND BLACK PEPPER, TO TASTE

Slice the leeks into rounds, then wash very thoroughly. Drain and place in a pot with remaining ingredients. Simmer gently for 30-40 minutes or until tender. Serve garnished with a little fresh mint.

FAMILY PEAS – *Petits Pois à la Demi Bourgeoise*

1 kg FRESH PEAS

1 LETTUCE, WASHED AND SHREDDED

2 SHALLOTS

PINCH VEGISALT

3 TABLESPOONS BUTTER

1 SPRIG PARSLEY

1 TEASPOON BROWN SUGAR

3 TABLESPOONS CREAM

Place peas and butter in a pot and stew gently for 20 minutes. Add lettuce, parsley, shallots and sugar and continue to cook for another 15-20 minutes. Season to taste with salt and remove from heat. Stir in cream, reheat but do not boil, then serve at once.

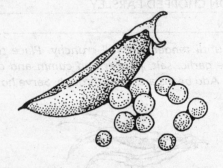

ONIONS WITH GARLIC – *Oignons à L'Ail*

4 LARGE ONIONS

10-12 CLOVES GARLIC

PINCH VEGISALT

FRESHLY GROUND BLACK PEPPER

3 TABLESPOONS OLIVE OIL

SMALL SPRIG ROSEMARY

Peel the onions and then plunge them into boiling water for 20 minutes. Add the whole cloves of garlic and continue to simmer for a further 5 minutes. Remove onions and garlic from the water and hollow out the centres of the onions. Place onion centres, garlic, salt, pepper and oil in a blender to purée or, alternatively, pound in a mortar with a pestle. Stuff the onions with the garlic mixture and place in a buttered baking dish. Bake in a moderate (350°F/180°C) oven with the rosemary for 30-35 minutes or until golden brown.

ROASTED EGGPLANT – *Aubergines en Gigot*

4 MEDIUM SIZED EGGPLANTS

4 RASHERS BACON, DICED (OPTIONAL)

20 CLOVES GARLIC

PINCH VEGISALT

FRESHLY GROUND BLACK PEPPER

1 TEASPOON FRESH BASIL, FINELY CHOPPED

1 TEASPOON FRESH OREGANO, FINELY CHOPPED

4 TABLESPOONS OLIVE OIL

Keeping the eggplant whole, make two rows of small incisions along the lengths of the eggplants. Fill these with pieces of bacon and whole cloves of garlic, which may be sliced lengthwise if they are very large. Sprinkle with salt, pepper and herbs and then place in an oiled baking dish. Drizzle with olive oil and roast in a low (325°/170°) oven for 1 hour.

GREEN SALAD – *Salade Verte*

LETTUCE – MIGNONETTE, COS, RADDICHIO, ICEBERG

DANDELION GREENS

CHICORY GREENS

CURLY ENDIVE

VINAIGRETTE

Mix together all or some of the above greens and toss in a light vinaigrette. Green Salad can be garnished with a mixture of herbs, such as parsley, chives, chervil and celery leaves.

VINEGAR DRESSING – *Sauce Vinaigrette*

3 TABLESPOONS COLD PRESSED SALAD OIL

1 TABLESPOON LEMON JUICE

1 TABLESPOON WHITE WINE VINEGAR

1 CLOVE GARLIC, CRUSHED

½ TEASPOON FRESH TARRAGON

½ TEASPOON FRESH CHERVIL

1 TEASPOON FRESH BASIL, FINELY CHOPPED

PINCH VEGISALT

FRESHLY GROUND BLACK PEPPER

½ TEASPOON HONEY

½ TEASPOON FRENCH MUSTARD

Place all ingredients in a glass jar. Screw the lid on tightly and shake well. Chill until required. This dressing keeps for 2-3 days in the fridge.

JAPANESE SALADE – *Salad Japonaise*

4 MEDIUM SIZED TOMATOES

100g FRESH CRAB MEAT

1 TEASPOON TOMATO PASTE

PINCH CAYENNE PEPPER

2 CARROTS, FINELY GRATED

8 PRAWNS, SHELLED (OPTIONAL)

½ GRAPEFRUIT

2 TABLESPOONS SOYA MAYONNAISE

1 TABLESPOON YOGHURT

100g ALFALFA SPROUTS

CURLY ENDIVE

Slice tops off tomatoes and set aside. Hollow out tomatoes and place flesh in a bowl. Peel grapefruit, discard seeds and pith, and dice. Place diced grapefruit in bowl with tomato and crab meat. In another bowl, mix together mayonnaise, tomato paste, yoghurt and cayenne until smooth. Use half this mixture to dress the crab which should then be piled into the tomatoes. Replace tomato lids, using miniature umbrella-shaped cocktail sticks to secure. Place stuffed tomatoes on a bed of endive and garnish with alfalfa sprouts and carrot. Dip prawns into remaining dressing and arrange around stuffed tomatoes. Serve chilled.

MARINATED FIGS – *Figues Marines*

12 FRESH OR DRIED FIGS

2 TABLESPOONS BRANDY

125ml APPLE JUICE

2 TABLESPOONS FLAKED ALMONDS

Place figs and apple juice in a pot. Bring to the boil and simmer for 1 minute. Remove from heat and stir in brandy. Allow to cool then refrigerate for at least 2 hours. Serve with yoghurt sweetened with a little maple syrup and garnish with flaked almonds.

BAKED BANANAS – *Bananes en Papillote*

4 MEDIUM-SIZED BANANAS

2 TABLESPOONS ORANGE JUICE

1 TEASPOON VANILLA ESSENCE

1 TEASPOON GRATED ORANGE RIND

1 TABLESPOON MAPLE SYRUP

2 TABLESPOONS CHOPPED WANUTS

Peel bananas and place each one on an individual sheet of aluminium foil. Mix together remaining ingredients and divide into 4 portions. Spoon a portion of orange juice mixture over each banana. Seal the aluminium foil and then bake bananas in a hot (425°F/220°C) oven for 20 minutes. Serve hot.

PINEAPPLE FLAMBÉ – *Ananas Flambé*

4 SLICES FRESH PINEAPPLE, PEELED AND CORED

4 TABLESPOONS WHITE RUM

2 TABLESPOONS RAISINS

2 TABLESPOONS CHOPPED WALNUTS

Place pineapple slices on a serving dish. Fill the centre of each slice with a mixture of raisins and walnuts. Warm the rum gently in a heavy pot then pour over the pineapple slices. Set the rum alight and serve at once.

CHEESE AND FRUIT – *Fruits et Fromages*

One of the best French desserts is a platter of cheese and fruit. Place cheese and fruits on a bed of watercress and serve cold.

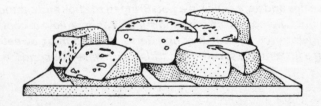

GREECE

Greek vegetarian cuisine may seem to be a contradiction in terms to some peope – Greek food without lamb? Without fish? It doesn't seem as if it would be authentic and yet there are hundreds of delicious and nutritious vegetarian dishes from Greece, from the famous dolmades (stuffed vine leaves) and spanakopita (spinach pie) to the less well-known salata kolokithaloulouda (zucchini flower salad).

Traditionally, observers of the Greek Orthodox faith follow a vegetarian diet over the period of Lent and so a great number of meatless recipes have been devised to maintain interest during that period – for the Greeks love to eat good food, whatever the time of year.

The diet is a healthy one with plenty of fresh vegetables and fruit as well as lentils, beans, millet and yoghurt. As with many other cuisines, the desserts are often sweet and sticky, based as they are on white sugar, so only three have been included here and they have been translated to honey as far as that is possible. Unless you have a very sweet tooth, it is probably more satisfying to end a Greek meal with fresh fruit, such as figs or grapes rather than with baklava or custard pie. It is certainly better for your health anyway!

DIPS

Serve these dips with wholemeal bread, raw vegetables such as sticks of carrot, celery or cucumber, or as a side dish with the main meal.

EGG PLANT DIP – *Melitzanosalata*

2 LARGE EGGPLANTS

60 g FETA CHEESE, CRUMBLED

½ CUP NATURAL YOGHURT

1 CUP OLIVE OIL

1 LEMON, JUICED

3 CLOVES GARLIC, CRUSHED

PINCH CAYENNE PEPPER

PINCH SEA SALT

Wash eggplants and place on an oiled baking tray in a moderate oven – 180°C (350°F). Cook for 1½ hours or until soft. Cut the eggplants in half and remove the pulp. Blend it in a food processor or use a mortar and pestle, gradually adding remaining ingredients until the mixture is thick and creamy. Chill and garnish with a little extra cayenne pepper just before serving.

CUCUMBER – YOGHURT DIP – *Tzatsiki*

1 LARGE OR TWO SMALL CUCUMBERS, PEELED AND SLICED

1 CUP NATURAL YOGHURT

2 CLOVES GARLIC, CRUSHED

1 TABLESPOON FRESH MINT, FINELY CHOPPED

1 TABLESPOON FRESH PARLSEY, FINELY CHOPPED

1 TEASPOON WHITE WINE VINEGAR

SEA SALT AND FRESHLY GROUND BLACK PEPPER, TO TASTE

1 EXTRA SPRIG MINT FOR GARNISH

PINCH PAPRIKA

Sprinkle cucumber with salt and place in a colander. Leave for 20 minutes to drain, then pat dry with absorbent paper. Meanwhile, combine remaining ingredients except for the extra sprig of mint and paprika. Pour the yoghurt mixture over the cucumber and stir well. Place in a serving dish and chill. Just before serving sprinkle with paprika and garnish with fresh mint.

LENTIL SOUP – *Soupa Fakes*

1½ CUPS BROWN LENTILS

6 TABLESPOONS OLIVE OIL

1 LARGE ONION, CHOPPED

2 CLOVES GARLIC, CRUSHED

2 MEDIUM CARROTS, SLICED INTO ROUNDS

500g TOMATOES, SKINNED AND CHOPPED

1 TABLESPOON FRESH PARSLEY, FINELY CHOPPED

PINCH OREGANO

SEA SALT AND FRESHLY GROUND BLACK PEPPER, TO TASTE

2 TABLESPOONS CIDER VINEGAR

Soak lentils overnight. Next day, bring them to the boil, then change the water. In a pan, heat the oil and fry the onion and garlic for 5 minutes. Add the carrots, tomatoes and rinsed lentils, stirring all the while to prevent sticking. Add 4 cups cold water, bring to the boil then reduce to simmer for 45 minutes. The vegetables should be cooked but not mushy. When cooked, add parsley and oregano and season with salt and pepper to taste. Add vinegar to individual dishes just before serving.

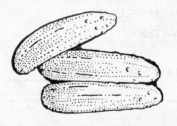

SAUCES

Greek cooking depends quite a bit on the use of sauces. The two which appear below are very versatile and can be used with a great variety of dishes.

BECHAMEL SAUCE – *Saltsa Bessamel*

3 TABLESPOONS BUTTER

½ SMALL ONION, FINELY CHOPPED

3 TABLESPOONS WHOLEMEAL FLOUR

500 ml HOT MILK

6 BLACK PEPPERCORNS

1 SMALL BAY LEAF

PINCH SEA SALT

PINCH NUTMEG

4 EGG YOLKS

250 g PARMESAN CHEESE, FINELY GRATED

In the top of a double boiler, melt the butter and cook the onion. Stir in the flour then gradually add the hot milk, beating all the while. Add peppercorns, bay leaf, salt and nutmeg and cook for 10-15 minutes, stirring regularly. Strain the sauce through a fine sieve and beat in the four egg yolks and grated cheese away from heat.

LEMON SAUCE – *Saltsa Lemoni*

Use this sauce to accompany dolmades or other stuffed vegetables, rich dishes or fish.

1½ TEASPOONS CORNFLOUR

200 ml BOILING WATER

2 EGGS

1 LARGE OR 2 SMALL LEMONS, JUICED

PINCH SEA SALT

Dissolve the cornflour in a little cold water then add boiling water. Boil for 1 minute then leave to cool while you prepare the other ingredients. Separate the eggs, discarding one of the whites (or reserving it for later use in another dish). Beat together the yolks, the remaining egg white, lemon juice and salt, then gradually add the cornflour mixture, beating constantly. Return to heat and continue beating until the sauce thickens but do not boil. Serve at once.

SALADS

GREEK SALAD

1 CRISP LETTUCE

1 MEDIUM CUCUMBER

2 TOMATOES, CUT IN WEDGES

1 ONION, FINELY SLICED

100g BLACK OLIVES

100g GREEN OLIVES

250g FETA CHEESE

PINCH OREGANO

½ CUP OLIVE OIL

2 TABLESPOONS WHITE WINE

2 TABLESPOONS CIDER VINEGAR

PINCH SEA SALT

FRESHLY GROUND BLACK PEPPER

6 ANCHOVY FILLETS

Wash the lettuce and tear into bit-size pieces. Pile into a large salad bowl. Peel and slice the cucumber thickly and, together with the tomatoes and olives, add to the lettuce. Cut the feta cheese into cubes and add most to the salad, reserving a few for garnish. In a separate bowl, combine oregano, oil, vinegar, salt and pepper. Drizzle the dressing over the salad and then garnish with anchovy fillets and reserved feta.

CAULIFLOWER SALAD – *Kounoupidi*

1 SMALL CAULIFLOWER
½ CUP OLIVE OIL
1 LEMON, JUICE
¼ TEASPOON HONEY
PINCH SEA SALT
3 BLACK OLIVES, STONED AND CHOPPED
PINCH BLACK PEPPER
PINCH MUSTARD POWDER

Break the cauliflower into flowerettes and steam lightly. This will take 5-7 minutes. The cauliflower should be crunchy, and while it is cooking, place all the remaining ingredients in a glass jar, screw the lid on tightly and shake vigorously. Drizzle this dressing over the cooked cauliflower and serve warm or cold.

VEGETABLE DISHES

STUFFED ARTICHOKES – *Agginares Gemistes*

6 GLOBE ARTICHOKES
3 CUPS GREEK RICE (SEE BELOW)

Cook the artichokes in boiling water until tender – about 20 minutes. Drain and leave to cool. When cool enough to handle, pull out the centre leaf. Scoop the choke ('hairy beard') out of the centre with a teaspoon but take care to leave the heart intact. Fan out the leaves and fill each artichoke with half a cup of Greek Rice. Cover and bake in a medium oven 180°C (350°F) for 20 minutes. Serve with Lemon Sauce and a salad.

SPINACH PIE – *Spanakopita*

1 BUNCH (1 kg) FRESH SPINACH OR SILVER BEET

1 TABLESPOON OLIVE OIL

1 LARGE ONION, FINELY CHOPPED

12 SHALLOTS, FINELY CHOPPED

4 EGGS, LIGHTLY BEATEN

500 g FETA CHEESE, CRUMBLED

3 TABLESPOONS FRESH PARSLEY, FINELY CHOPPED

PINCH OREGANO

PLENTY OF FRESHLY GROUND BLACK PEPPER

PINCH CINNAMON

PINCH NUTMEG

375 g FILO PASTRY

125 g MELTED BUTTER

Wash spinach thoroughly then put into a pan without any extra water. The water clinging to the leaves will be enough to cook the spinach in. Cook over a low heat for about 5 minutes. Leave the lid on the pot – the spinach will wilt further while you are preparing the rest of the ingredients. In a large bowl, combine the onion and shallots which have been lightly sauteed in the oil with the eggs, feta cheese, parsley, oregano, pepper, cinnamon and nutmeg. Mix together very well. Chop the spinach roughly and then add to the mixture.

To assemble the spanakopita lay half the sheets of filo pastry on a buttered baking dish, butering every second sheet well. Top the pastry with the spinach mixture and then cover with the remaining sheets of pastry, again buttering every second sheet. Pour any extra melted butter over the top, fold in the ends of the pastry and bake at 190°C (375°F) for 45 minutes or until golden brown.

ZUCCHINI-FILLED VINE LEAVES – *Kolokithya Dolmades*

Fresh vine leaves are not available in the autumn, so tinned ones will have to be used if you wish to make these dolmades now. In the spring, however, you can use tender young leaves fresh from the vine.

4 TABLESPOONS OLIVE OIL

1 LARGE ONION, FINELY CHOPPED

4 MEDIUM-SIZED ZUCCHINI, FINELY CHOPPED

½ CUP PINE NUTS

4 TOMATOES, SKINNED AND CHOPPED

½ LEMON, JUICED

1 TABLESPOON PARSLEY, FINELY CHOPPED

PINCH OREGANO

PINCH SEA SALT

FRESHLY GROUND BLACK PEPPER, TO TASTE

1 CUP COOKED LONG GRAIN BROWN RICE

40 VINE LEAVES, BLANCHED AND DRAINED

Heat oil and sauté onion and zucchini for 5 minutes. Add pine nuts and tomatoes and cook for a further 5 minutes. Remove from heat and add lemon juice, parsley, oregano, salt, pepper and rice. Stir well. Place a tablespoonful of this mixture into the centre of each vine leaf then roll up. Tuck in the end and pack tightly into a lightly greased pan. Cover with a little water and bake in a moderate (180°C/350°F) oven for 20 minutes. Serve hot with Lemon Sauce and a salad.

STUFFED CABBAGE – *Lahanodolmades*

16 CABBAGE LEAVES, BLANCHED AND DRAINED

1 LARGE OR 2 SMALL EGGPLANTS

2 CAPSICUMS, 1 RED AND 1 GREEN, FINELY CHOPPED

3 TABLESPOONS OLIVE OIL

1 CUP COOKED BROWN RICE

½ CUP PINE NUTS

1 CUP WATER

½ CUP WHITE WINE

1 LEMON, JUICED

2 TABLESPOONS OLIVE OIL

2 ONIONS, PEELED AND LEFT WHOLE

A FEW PEPPERCORNS

Blanch the cabbage leaves quickly in boiling water and leave to drain. Sauté the eggplants and capsicums in olive oil then add rice and nuts. Put a tablespoon of stuffing into the centre of each cabbage leaf then roll up. Tuck in the ends and pack tightly into a lightly greased pan. Cover with remaining ingredients. Bring to the boil, reduce to simmer and cover pot. Leave to cook over a low heat for 30 minutes. Remove onions and serve with a salad.

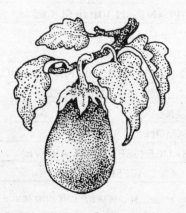

BEAN CASSEROLE – *Fassoulika*

These beans are equally good served hot with the main meal or cold as a salad.

500g RUNNER BEANS

1 CUP OLIVE OIL

500g TOMATOES, SKINNED AND CHOPPED

2 LARGE ONIONS, SLICED LENGTHWISE

4 LARGE POTATOES, QUARTERED

1 TEASPOON HONEY

PINCH SEA SALT

PLENTY OF FRESHLY GROUND BLACK PEPPER

APPROXIMATELY 4 CUPS WATER

Top, tail, string and slice the beans. Heat the oil and cook the onions until soft. Add all the remaining ingredients – there should be plenty of water. Bring to the boil, reduce to simmer, cover and cook until all the water has evaporated. This takes 45-60 minutes. Check from time to time to see whether more water is needed. When done the beans should be very soft indeed.

MOUSSAKA

Traditionally cooked with minced lamb, the meatless moussaka made with eggplants is also a very popular dish.

3 LARGE EGGPLANTS IN 10mm SLICES

2 TABLESPOONS OLIVE OIL

4 TABLESPOONS BUTTR

1 LARGE OR 2 SMALL ONIONS, FINELY CHOPPED

4 TOMATOES, SKINNED AND DICED

PINCH OREGANO

PINCH CINNAMON

BECHAMEL SAUCE (SEE RECIPE ABOVE)

100g PARMESAN CHEESE, GRATED

Sprinkle the eggplant slices with salt and leave to drain in a colander. Rinse and pat dry with absorbent paper. Sauté quickly in a lightly oiled pan and drain on absorbent paper. Set aside and make tomato sauce. Heat butter and sauté onions for 5 minutes. Add tomatoes, oregano and cinnamon and cook for a further 5 minutes. To assemble the moussaka lightly grease a deep baking dish. Put in a layer of eggplant on the bottom, top with tomato sauce and follow with bechamel sauce. Repeat the layers ending with bechamel. Sprinkle with grated parmesan and bake in a moderate oven 180°C (350°F) for 30 minutes or until golden brown.

GREEK RICE – *Rizi Hellenici*

Serve this rice as a filling for dolmades or vegetables such as artichokes, eggplants or tomatoes, on its own, with lemon sauce or as an accompaniment to the main meal.

2 TABLESPOONS OLIVE OIL
2 ONIONS, FINELY CHOPPED
2 CLOVES GARLIC, CRUSHED
2 STICKS CELERY, FINELY CHOPPED
2 TABLESPOONS ROASTED SESAME SEEDS
2 TABLESPOONS ROASTED SUNFLOWER SEEDS
2 TABLESPOONS PINE NUTS
2 CUPS COOKED BROWN RICE
2 TEASPOONS MINT, FINELY CHOPPED
2 TEASPOONS FRESHLY SQUEEZED LEMON JUICE
2 TABLESPOONS PARSLEY, FINELY CHOPPED
PINCH OREGANO
PINCH SEA SALT
FRESHLY GROUND BLACK PEPPER, TO TASTE

Heat the oil and saute onions and garlic till soft. Add celery, sesame and sunflower seeds and pine nuts and cook over a low light until the rice takes on a golden hue – this takes 5-10 minutes. Stir in the remaining ingredients and serve.

DESSERTS

Flan

3 WHOLE EGGS

3 EGG YOLKS

1/2 CUP WHITE SUGAR

2 CUPS MILK

A FEW DROPS VANILLA ESSENCE

SYRUP:
1/2 CUP WATER

1 CUP WHITE SUGAR

Beat the eggs and egg yolks, then add the sugar and beat again. Warm the milk – just to take the chill off – and add to the eggs. Mix in vanilla and leave. Meanwhile, heat 1/2 cup water and one full cup of sugar. Boil till it browns, then swirl this syrup around the bottom of the custard dish. Pour custard over syrup. Place the dish in a baking tin filled with water above the level of the custard. Bake for 1 hour in a slow oven – 150°C (300°F). Allow to cool and serve with cream and fruit or on its own.

Baklava

375g FILO PASTRY

250g UNSALTED BUTTER, MELTED

1 CUP ALMONDS, CHOPPED

1 TEASPOON CINNAMON

1 TEASPOON NUTMEG

1/3 CUP HONEY

SYRUP:
1 1/2 CUPS HONEY

1/2 CUP WATER

1 TEASPOON LEMON JUICE

1/2 TEASPOON LEMON RIND, GRATED

1 CINNAMON STICK

Lay half the sheets of filo pastry on a lightly greased baking tray, brushing every second sheet with the melted butter. Sprinkle the chopped almonds, cinnamon and nutmeg on the pastry, drizzle with honey and then cover with the remaining sheets of pastry, again brushing ever second sheet with melted butter. Trim the edges and cut the pastry into diamond shapes. Pour any remaining butter onto the pastry and bake in a moderate oven at 180°C (350°F) for 1 hour or until golden brown. Pour cold syrup over the hot baklava or hot syrup over cold. Traditionally served with tiny cups of very strong coffee and a glass of cold water.

GREEK CUSTARD ROLLS

375 g FILO PASTRY

200 g UNSALTED BUTTER, MELTED

FILLING:
4 CUPS MILK

2 EGG YOLKS, LIGHTLY BEATEN

3 TABLESPOONS CORNFLOUR

1 TABLESPOON CUSTARD POWDER

1 TABLESPOON SEMOLINA

1 TABLESPOON HONEY

1 TEASPOON VANILLA ESSENCE
TOPPING:
ICING SUGAR

NUTMEG

Take a sheet of filo pastry, brush with melted butter and fold in half lengthwise. Place 1 tablespoon of the filling on one end of the pastry and then roll up. Tuck in the ends, brush with melted butter and bake in a hot oven 200°C (400°F) for 40 minutes or until golden brown. Cool and sprinkle with a little icing sugar mixed with nutmeg.

Filling
Combine all filling ingredients over a low heat, stirring constantly till it thickens. Leave to cool for at least 15 minutes before using.

BRITAIN

There's more to British cooking than greasy fish and chips and stodgy puddings. At its best, British food is simple and tasty and, surprisingly, very healthful. The North Sea has traditionally offered an abundant supply of fish and other seafoods, while hedgerows are laden with plenty of berries in the summer months. Potatoes feature fairly heavily as a vegetable, as do delicious leeks, cabbage and watercress.

Vegetable dishes are not, however, a forté of British cuisine, so it is wise to add a fresh tossed salad to the following recipes wherever it is appropriate. Since Britain has become more integrated with the rest of Europe, vegetables are appearing on local menus more and more. A British salad is no longer composed of the mandatory limp lettuce leaf, grated cheese, soggy tomato and slice of beetroot. Now it is much more likely to comprise raddichio, cos, iceberg and herbs as these tasty greens have become incorporated into the British culinary repertoire over the last few years.

Desserts are a specialty in Britain – particularly those made with apples and berries since these fruits grow so well in Britain. Another popular ingredient, especially in Scottish desserts, is oatmeal. This is toasted and used as a crunchy topping or ground fine and made into biscuits which are served hot with butter and cheese.

British cheeses are a special delight. Try oatcakes and water biscuits (bought at delicatessens) with a mixed plate of Caerphilly, Cheddar, Cheshire, Double Gloucester, Wensleydale, Stilton, Derby Sage, Leicester and little pots of cottage cheese.

Finally, it is as well to remember that the most valuable ingredient of British cuisine is a good pinch of understatement. Good British food is never masked by strongly flavoured spices but rather relies on fresh produce cooked in a plain, unfussy manner.

COCK-A-LEEKIE

1 CHICKEN
6 LEEKS, WASHED AND SLICED
PLENTY OF FRESHLY GROUND BLACK PEPPER
2 TABLESPOONS FINELY CHOPPED PARSLEY
PRUNES, SOAKED IN WATER OVERNIGHT, TO GARNISH
1 LITRE WATER OR BEEF STOCK
1 TEASPOON VEGISALT

Place chicken in a large pot and cover with water or stock. Simmer for 1 hour or until the chicken is tender. Remove chicken from the bone and chop or slice. Discard bones and fat and set aside to cool. When cold, skim fat from the surface of the soup and discard or use in other dishes. Add leeks to the chicken broth and simmer for 15 minutes. Season to taste with vegisalt and black pepper. To serve, ladle hot soup into bowls and garnish with chopped parsley and 2 or 3 plump prunes.

HAMPSHIRE WATERCRESS SOUP

1 BUNCH WATERCRESS
1 ONION, FINELY CHOPPED
1 LITRE WATER
FRESHLY GRATED BLACK PEPPER
1 TABLESPOON LEMON JUICE
2 TABLESPOONS BUTTER
2 POTATOES, DICED
PINCH VEGISALT
PINCH NUTMEG
3 TABLESPOONS CREAM

Wash and trim watercress. Reserve a few sprigs for garnish then chop the rest. Melt butter and sauté onion for a few minutes until soft. Add potatoes, watercress, water and vegisalt and cover. Simmer for 30 minutes than purée the soup in a blender or push through a sieve. Return to pot and bring back to the boil. Stir in remaining ingredients and serve hot or cold.

HADDOCK SOUP – *Cullen skink* (Scotland)

500g SMOKED HADDOCK (OR SIMILAR)

4 POTATOES, QUARTERED

1 LITRE MILK, SIMMERING

FRESHLY GROUND BLACK PEPPER

FRESH BROWN TOAST

500ml WATER

1 ONION, CHOPPED

PINCH NUTMEG

2 TABLESPOONS PARSLEY, FINELY CHOPPED

Place fish and water in a pan and bring to the boil. Add potatoes and onion, cover and reduce to simmer for 25-30 minutes. Drain fish and potatoes and mash or blend in a food processor with 1 cup milk. Blend until smooth then add soup to remaining hot milk. Season with nutmeg and pepper and continue to cook over a low heat for 5 minutes. Garnish with parsley and serve with slices of freshly made toast.

BALLYMALOE BROWN BREAD (Ireland)

500g STONEGROUND WHOLEMEAL FLOUR

1 PACKET DRIED YEAST

350ml TEPID WATER

2 TEASPOONS SALT

1 TABLESPOON BLACK TREACLE

Warm the flour and salt in a very low oven. Stir in the yeast and set aside. Dissolve the treacle in half the tepid water and stir into the flour. Add enough of the remaining water to make a fairly wet dough. Since this bread is not kneaded, the dough is usually quite sticky. You may need a little extra water to get the right consistency. Place the dough in a buttered bread tin and cover with a plastic bag. Tie the bag so that it is airtight and leave in a warm place to rise. This takes about 45 minutes. The mixture will not double in quantity as yeasted breads do, so don't think you've done anything wrong when you return to the dough. Place in a hot oven (230°C/450°F) for 40 minutes. Remove and brush the top with water. Put back into the oven for 5 minutes, then remove and turn out to cool on a wire rack.

FLOUNDER IN CIDER (Cornwall)

6 SHALLOTS, FINELY CHOPPED

PINCH VEGISALT

1 CUP CIDER

1 TABLESPOON LEMON JUICE

2 TABLESPOONS FLOUR

4 TABLESPOONS PARMESAN CHEESE, FRESHLY GRATED

4 FILLETS FLOUNDER

FRESHLY GROUND BLACK PEPPER

1 GREEN APPLE, PEELED AND SLICED

2 TABLESPOONS BUTTER

3 TABLESPOONS CREAM

Place shallots in a buttered baking dish. Cover with flounder fillets and season with salt and pepper. Carefully pour on cider and lemon juice and arrange apple slices on fish. Cover dish with tin foil and bake in a moderate (350°F/180°C) oven for 10-15 minutes. Remove fish and set aside to keep warm. Strain the liquid. Melt butter, stir in flour and cook for 1 minute then gradually add hot fish liquid, stirring all the time to make a thick, glossy sauce. Stir in the cream then pour sauce over fish. Sprinkle with grated parmesan cheese and place under a hot griller for 3-4 minutes or until golden and bubbly. Serve hot.

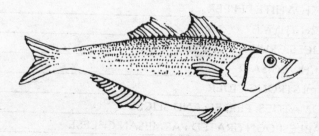

GREENWICH FISH STEW

1 kg FIRM WHITE FISH FILLETS

500 g FRESH CRAB MEAT

2 TOMATOES, SKINNED AND CHOPPED

1 SMALL LEMON, CUT INTO QUARTERS

5-7 BLACK PEPPERCORNS

1 TABLESPOONS PARSLEY, ROUGHLY CHOPPED

3 TABLESPOONS OLIVE OIL

500 g PRAWNS, COOKED AND PEELED

3 ONIONS, SLICED

3 CLOVES GARLIC, CRUSHED

PINCH VEGISALT

1 BAY LEAF

PINCH SAFFRON

Cut fish into bite-sized pieces. Devein prawns and cut up if small or leave whole if preferred. Heat oil and add onion slices. Sauté for 5 minutes then add seafood. Stir well, then pour in just enough water to cover. Bring to boil then add tomato, garlic, lemon, vegisalt, peppercorns and bay leaf. Reduce heat and simmer very gently for 15 minutes. Add chopped parsley and saffron and continue to cook for 2-3 minutes. Remove bay leaf and lemon and serve hot.

CORNISH CHICKEN

4 CHICKEN BREASTS

PINCH WHITE PEPPER

PINCH THYME

4 SLICES GRUYÈRE CHEESE

PINCH VEGISALT

500 ml STRONG CIDER

4 TOMATOES, PEELED AND SLICED

1 TABLESPOON GRATED PARMESAN CHEESE

Rub chicken breasts with salt and pepper and place in a pot. Cover with cider, bring to the boil then reduce to simmer for 20-30 minutes or until cooked. Remove chicken and place on an oven-proof serving plate. Top each chicken breast with slices of tomato and a slice of cheese. Sprinkle with parmesan cheese and place under a hot griller for 5 minutes or until golden. Serve immediately.

WELSH CHICKEN

1 CHICKEN

2 LEEKS, WASHED AND SLICED

3 TABLESPOONS FLOUR

1 SPRIG THYME

2 TABLESPOONS PARSLEY, FINELY CHOPPED

FRESHLY GROUND BLACK PEPPER, TO TASTE

5 RASHERS BACON

3 CARROTS, SLICED

1 SMALL CABBAGE, SHREDDED

PINCH OREGANO

PINCH VEGISALT

500 ml CHICKEN STOCK

Wash the chicken thoroughly and then truss it ready for cooking. Fry bacon until crisp then remove from pan. Crumble bacon and reserve. Discard all but 2 tablespoons of the bacon fat then sauté leeks and carrots in it for 5-10 minutes or until soft. Stir in the flour, cook for 1 minute, then add crumbled bacon, cabbage, thyme, oregano, parsley, salt, pepper and stock. Bring to boil then add the chicken. Reduce to simmer over a very low light for 2 hours. Remove chicken from casserole and place on a serving dish. Remove cabbage from pot with a slotted spoon and arrange around chicken. Pour some of the sauce onto the chicken and serve the rest separately.

LINCOLNSHIRE STOVIES

| 1 kg POTATOES |
| 500 ml CHICKEN STOCK |
| 3 TABLESPOONS FLOUR |
| PINCH VEGISALT |
| 1 TEASPOON SAGE, FINELY CHOPPED |
| 2 ONIONS, SLICED |
| 3 TABLESPOONS BUTTER |
| 500 ml MILK |
| PEPPER, TO TASTE |
| 2 TABLESPOONS TASTY CHEESE, GRATED |

Place the potatoes in a pot of boiling water and simmer until almost cooked. Remove from pot, allow to cool slightly, then peel and slice. Place onion and potato slices in alternate layers in a buttered dish, ending with a layer of onions. Heat butter and stir in flour, cook in 1 minute then gradually add hot milk to form a sauce. Stir in chicken stock and pour this mixture over the potatoes and onions. Season to taste with salt and pepper, sprinkle with sage and top with cheese. Bake in a hot (400°F/ 200°C) oven for 15-20 minutes or until slightly brown and crunchy.

IRISH POTATO PANCAKES – *Boxty*

| 750 g POTATOES |
| 250 g WHOLEMEAL FLOUR |
| BUTTER AND/OR OIL, FOR FRYING |
| PINCH SALT |
| MILK |

Boil half the potatoes until soft. Peel and mash. Peel remaining potatoes and grate. Squeeze out as much excess liquid as possible then add to cooked, mashed potatoes. Work in salt and flour then add as much milk as required to make a thick batter. The amount varies according to the starchiness of the potatoes. Heat butter and/or oil and fry spoonfuls of potato mixture as you would pikelets. Fry both sides until golden and crisp and serve hot.

OATCAKES

1½ CUPS FINELY GROUND OATMEAL

½ TEAPSOON BAKING POWDER

2-3 TABLESPOONS HOT WATER

PINCH SALT

2 TABLESPOONS MELTED BUTTER

Place oatmeal in a bowl with the salt and baking powder. Stir in the melted butter and add just enough water to make a stiff dough. Sprinkle a board with a little extra oatmeal and roll out dough until it is 3-4 mm thick. Cut into rounds with a cookie cutter and place on a greased baking sheet. Bake in a moderate (350°F/ 180°C) oven for 20 minutes then turn the oven off but leave the oatcakes for an extra 5 minutes before removing. Serve hot with butter and cheese.

BROWN BREAD ICE CREAM

750 ml CREAM

1 VANILLA POD

100 g BROWN SUGAR

¼ CUP FRESH BROWN BREADCRUMBS

Pour one quarter or almost 200 ml of the cream into a pot. Add sugar and vanilla pod and simmer until sugar dissolves, stirring constantly. Remove vanilla pod, scraping the seeds back into the cream. Allow to cool. Meanwhile, beat the rest of the cream until stiff. Fold beaten cream and breadcrumbs into sweetened cream, stirring well, then pour into ice cream trays. Place in freezer compartment of fridge, taking out and stirring every couple of hours to prevent ice crystals from forming. Serve with raspberries, peaches or bananas.

RICE PUDDING

½ CUP BROWN RICE
1½ CUPS MILK
1 TEASPOON VANILLA ESSENCE
½ CUP DARK BROWN SUGAR
PINCH CINNAMON
2 CUPS BOILING WATER
3 TABLESPOONS HONEY
4 EGG YOLKS
1 CUP CREAM

Place rice in a pot and cover with boiling water. Simmer for 5 minutes then strain. Return rice to pot and add milk and honey. Cover and simmer gently for 45 minutes or until all the milk has been absorbed and the rice is tender. Cool the rice and then stir in the vanilla essence. Place egg yolks, brown sugar and cream in the top of a double boiler and cook until the mixture thickens into a custard. This takes 10 minutes or so, and you need to stir the egg yolks frequently while they are cooking. Fold the rice into the custard and pile into a serving dish. Sprinkle with cinnamon and chill for several hours before serving.

HIGHLAND FLUMMERY

1 TABLESPOON OATMEAL
1 TABLESPOON SCOTCH WHISKY
2 TEASPOONS FRESHLY SQUEEZED LEMON JUICE
175 ml CREAM
3 TABLESPOONS HONEY

Toast the oatmeal in a heavy pan until light brown. Beat the cream until it is thick then stir in the whisky, honey and lemon juice. Mix well and spoon into individual serving dishes. Sprinkle with toasted oatmeal and serve.

BURNT CREAM

250 ml MILK

½ TEASPOON VANILLA EXTRACT

2 TABLESPOONS HONEY

2 TABLESPOON BROWN SUGAR

250 ml CREAM

4 EGG YOLKS

1 TABLESPOON BRANDY

Heat the milk, cream and vanilla over a very low light. Place egg yolks and honey in a large ovenproof dish and beat until thick and creamy. Stir in the brandy and hot milk mixture. Place dish in a bain-marie (larger pan or water) and cook in a low (300°F/150°C) oven for 1 hour or until the custard is set. Allow to cool then sprinkle with brown sugar and place under a hot griller for a few minutes until the top is dark brown and caramelised. Serve at once.

BLACKBERRY AND APPLE PIE

1 SWEET SHORTCRUST PIE CRUST

500 g GREEN APPLES, PEELED AND SLICED

PINCH NUTMEG

1 TABLESPOON MILK

2 PUNNETS BLACKBERRIES

1 TABLESPOON BROWN SUGAR

PINCH CINNAMON

Bake the pie crust for 10 minutes. Remove from oven and fill with blackberries and thinly sliced apples. Sprinkle with sugar, nutmeg and cinnamon and top with remaining pastry. Make two small slits in the top of the pie with a sharp knife. Brush the top with milk and sprinkle with a little extra sugar. Bake in a hot (400°F/200°C) oven for 25-30 minutes or until golden. Serve hot with custard, cream or yoghurt.

RASPBERRY FOOL

2 PUNNETS RASPBERRIES

2 TABLESPOONS SUGAR

1 CUP WHIPPED CREAM

1 TABLESPOON ROSE WATER

Mash raspberries until soft and then push through a sieve. Stir in sugar and rose water, mixing well. Gently fold in cream and pile into a serving dish. This looks very good decorated with almond slivers.

CREAM CHOWDIE (SCOTLAND)

1 CUP OATMEAL

3 TABLESPOONS HONEY

2 TABLESPOONS RUM

1 CUP CREAM

1 TEASPOON VANILLA ESSENCE

1 PUNNET RASPBERRIES

Place the oatmeal in a heavy frying pan and toast over a medium heat for 10-15 minutes, stirring all the time, until lightly browned. Set oatmeal aside to cool. Whip cream until stiff. Stir in honey, vanilla and rum and beat again. Fold in oatmeal and raspberries and chill for several hours before serving.

GERMANY

The Teutonic tradition with regard to eating is nothing if not robust. Germans often have five meals a day – not snacks, but entire meals! Breakfast is usually a hearty affair consisting of cooked eggs and meats, cheese, dark bread, rolls and coffee. This is followed by a second breakfast at mid-morning featuring a variety of meat and cheese sandwiches, sausages, rolls and salads and, a couple of hours later, the main meal of the day – lunch.

Lunch usually begins with piping hot soup and dumplings or noodles in winter or a cool, refreshing fruit soup in summer. This is followed by a meat or fish main course accompanied by various vegetables and salads and, always the ubiquitous potato. After the main course comes a fruit dessert or sweet omelette perhaps. A short rest follows before an enormous afternoon tea of sandwiches, cakes and coffee appears and then finally, if there is any room left, a light evening meal of bread, cheese and cold meats is enjoyed with a glass of white wine such as Reisling or Moselle or a stein of the famous German lager.

Fortunately, given the quantity, the quality of German food is usually very good. Tasty white asparagus, cauliflower and potatoes, deep red cabbage, tomatoes and beets, fresh cold-water seafoods and a stunning variety of dairy produce and whole grain breads form the basis of this healthy, if somewhat overwhelming, diet.

The main thing to remember with German food is to enjoy what you eat. Anyone who has ever tucked into a fabulous rich German pastry and a piping hot mug of cocoa will testify that it is easy to work up a 'Guten appetit' in this land of plenty.

ASPARAGUS SOUP – *Spargelsuppe*

The white, rather than green, variety of asparagus is used for this recipe.

500g WHITE ASPARAGUS

3 TABLESPOONS BUTTER

2 TABLESPOONS CREAM

PINCH NUTMEG

1 LITRE BOILING WATER

3 TABLESPOONS FLOUR

1 EGG YOLK

Wash asparagus and cut into 25mm (1" pieces). Simmer in boiling, salted water until tender. Melt butter and stir in flour. Cook for 1 minute then gradually add some of the asparagus water. When smooth, stir this mixture into the asparagus soup. Beat egg yolk until creamy. Add cream, stirring well then pour slowly into the hot soup. Serve hot garnished with nutmeg.

BERLIN LENTIL SOUP – *Linsensuppe Berlin*

250g LENTILS

3 RASHERS BACON

1 ONION, FINELY CHOPPED

1 POTATO, DICED

FRESHLY GROUND BLACK PEPPER

PINCH VEGISALT

SPRIG THYME

2 CARROTS, CHOPPED

2 TABLESPOONS FRESH LEMON JUICE

Soak lentils in water overnight. Next day bring to the boil, boil for 2 minutes, then turn heat off. Cover and leave to stand for 1 hour. Drain lentils. Chop bacon and sauté till crisp. Remove and set aside. Sauté onion, carrots and potato for a few minutes. Add thyme, lentils, vegisalt and bacon and cover with water. Cover and simmer gently for 3 hours. To serve, correct seasoning, adding lemon juice and plenty of freshly ground black pepper.

CELERY SALAD – *Selleriesalat*

2 LARGE KNOBS CELERY – WITHOUT STALKS

PINCH VEGISALT

3 TABLESPOONS OLIVE OIL

2 TABLESPOONS PARSLEY, CHOPPED

1 SMALL ONION, FINELY CHOPPED

PINCH PEPPER

3 TABLESPOONS CIDER VINEGAR

1 CUP CHICKEN STOCK

Wash celery and cook in boiling, salted water until tender. Drain, reserving liquid for stock. Chop celery. Combine pepper, vegisalt, vinegar, oil, chicken stock. parsley and onion and pour over the warm celery. Leave to stand for several hours, tossing occasionally to mix the flavours. Serve at room temperature.

POTATO PANCAKES – *Kartoffelpuffer*

750g POTATOES

2 EGGS, BEATEN

PINCH VEGISALT

3 TABLESPOONS OIL

1 SMALL ONION, GRATED

175g WHOLEMEAL FLOUR

3 TABLESPOONS BUTTER

BLACK PEPPER

Coarsely grate potatoes into a bowl. Add onion and egg yolks. Mix well then stir in flour and vegisalt. Heat enough of the butter and oil to grease the pan and cook pancakes a few at a time. The trick is not to overcrowd them. Take 2-3 tablespoons of potato mixture and flatten into cakes about 10cm (4") across. Cook until crisp and golden then turn and cook reverse side. Serve with plenty of salt and freshly ground black pepper. Or, if you prefer, serve in German style with berries or apple sauce.

SWABIAN CHEESE NOODLES – *Käsespätzle Swabia*

3 TABLESPOONS BUTTER
3 TABLESPOONS GRATED EMMENTHALER CHEESE
1 TEASPOON DRY MUSTARD POWDER
2 TABLESPOONS CHOPPED CHIVES
3 ONIONS, SLICED INTO RINGS
2 CUPS COOKED NOODLES

Melt butter and sauté onion rings for 5 minutes. Combine cheese and mustard. Add cooked noodles to cooked onions and cheese, mixing well. Place in a buttered ovenproof dish and bake in a low (300°F/150°C) oven for 25-30 minutes or until golden. Garnish with chives and serve hot.

POTATO AND TOMATO CASSEROLE –
Kartoffeln mit Tomaten

1 kg POTATOES, COOKED
3 TABLESPOONS GRATED CHEDDAR CHEESE
FRESHLY GROUND BLACK PEPPER
1 ONION, SLICED INTO RINGS AND SAUTÉED IN BUTTER
500 g TOMATOES, SLICED
PINCH VEGISALT
PINCH MARJORAM

Slice potatoes and arrange in a buttered casseroles in alternate layers with tomatoes and grated cheese. Sprinkle each layer with seasoning and marjoram and finish with a layer of onion rings and cheese. Bake in a moderate (350°F/180°C) oven for 30 minutes.

FISH SALAD – *Fischsalat*

500 g WHITE FISH FILLETS, COOKED AND FLAKED

1 TABLESPOON WINE VINEGAR

2-3 TABLESPOONS CHICKEN OR VEGETABLE STOCK

1 TEASPOON FRENCH MUSTARD

1 TEASPOON CHOPPED DILL

LEMON SLICES, TO GARNISH

2 TABLESPOONS SOYA MAYONNAISE

1 CLOVE GARLIC, CRUSHED

1 TABLESPOON CHOPPED PARSLEY

Place flaked fish in a bowl and cover with dressing. To make dressing, place vinegar, mayonnaise, stock, mustard, garlic and dill in a bowl. Mix well, correcting seasoning with a little vegisalt and cayenne pepper, if necessary. Fold fish into dressing and pile into a serving dish. Serve chilled or at room temperature, garnished with chopped parsley and a few slices of lemon.

BLUE TROUT – *Forelle Blau*

Only the freshest trout should be used for this recipe.

4 FRESH TROUT, CLEANED AND GUTTED

1 LITRE WATER

1 TEASPOON SALT

PARSLEY SPRIGS TO GARNISH

3 TABLESPOONS WHITE WINE

125 ml VINEGAR

1 LEMON, CUT INTO WEDGES

Place trout on a wet plate. Heat vinegar and pour over fish. This process changes their colour to blue. Leave to stand for 5 minutes. Combine water, wine and salt and simmer trout gently for 15 minutes. Remove with a slotted spoon and arrange on a hot serving dish. Garnish with lemon and parsley and serve with tiny new potatoes tossed in butter and parsley and a horseradish sauce.

HORSERADISH SAUCE – *Meerrettichsosse*

1 CUP WHIPPED CREAM

2 TABLESPOONS GRATED HORSERADISH

PINCH VEGISALT

¼ TEASPOON SUGAR

1 TEASPOON LEMON JUICE

PINCH CAYENNE PEPPER

Combine all ingredients, mixing well and serve cold with fish.

FISH WITH DILL – *Fischfillets in Dillsosse*

1 ONION, SLICED

1 BOUQUET GARNI

1 kg WHITE FISH FILLETS

1 SMALL ONION, FINELY CHOPPED

2 TABLESPOONS FRESH DILL, CHOPPED

3 TABLESPOONS MILK

PINCH SUGAR

500 ml WATER

2 TEASPOONS VEGISALT

2 TABLESPOONS BUTTER

2 TABLESPOONS FLOUR

2 TABLESPOONS CHOPPED PARSLEY

1 TEASPOON LEMON JUICE

PINCH CAYENNE PEPPER

Place onion in boiling water. Add bouquet garni, vegisalt and fish and simmer gently for 10 minutes. Meanwhile, heat butter and sauté onion till soft. Stir in flour and cook for 1 minute. Gradually add fish liquid to make a sauce the consistency of cream. Stir in herbs, milk, lemon juice, sugar and cayenne pepper and continue to cook over a low heat for 2 minutes. Pour hot sauce over fish and serve at once.

BAKED FLOUNDER – *Flundern Gebacken*

1 kg FLOUNDER FILLETS

1 LEMON, JUICED

BREADCRUMBS

SEA SALT

3 TABLESPOONS MILK

PARSLEY AND LEMON

Rub flounder with salt, sprinkle with lemon juice and dip in milk. Roll in breadcrumbs and sauté gently in a lightly buttered pan. Garnish with sprigs of parsley and wedges of lemon.

RED CABBAGE WITH APPLE – *Rotkohl mit Äpfeln*

1 SMALL RED CABBAGE, SHREDDED

2 TABLESPOONS DARK BROWN SUGAR

1 TABLESPOON BUTTER

3 MEDIUM APPLES, PEELED AND SLICED

3 BLACK PEPPERCORNS

SALT AND PEPPER TO TASTE

125 ml RED WINE

4 TABLESPOON RED WINE VINEGAR

3 LARGE ONIONS, SLICED

1 TABLESPOON VEGETABLE OIL

3 CLOVES

250 ml CHICKEN OR VEGETABLE STOCK

A FEW CARAWAY SEEDS

Combine cabbage, vinegar and sugar. Sauté onions in butter and oil. Place cabbage, onions and apples in alternate layers in a large casserole. Pour in remaining ingredients and simmer very slowly for 4 hours, stirring occasionally. Check moisture and seasoning from time to time, adding more stock if necessary. Serve hot.

BAVARIAN BEETS – *Rote Rüben*

500g BEETROOT, COOKED

1 TABLESPOON CHOPPED PARSLEY

2 CLOVES GARLIC, CRUSHED

1 TABLESPOON VINEGAR

3 TABLESPOONS BUTTER

1 TABLESPOON CHOPPED CHIVES

1 TEASPOON FLOUR

SALT AND PEPPER TO TASTE

Peel and slice beetroot. Melt butter and add herbs, garlic and flour. Cook for 1 minute then gradually add vinegar and seasoning. Add beetroot and simmer gently for 20 minutes. Serve hot or cold.

MOLASSES BREAD – *Weizenkeimbrot*

250g WHOLEMEAL FLOUR

2 TABLESPOONS BROWN SUGAR

1 CUP DARK RAISINS

2 CUPS BUTTERMILK (OR MILK)

125g WHEATGERM

PINCH VEGISALT

2 TEASPOONS BAKING POWDER

3 TABLESPOONS MOLASSES

Mix together flour, wheatgerm, sugar, vegisalt and raisins. In a separate bowl, combine baking powder, buttermilk and molasses. Pour the bubbling mixture into the dry ingredients and mix well. Spoon batter into a buttered loaf tin and bake at 325°F/160°C for 1 hour or until the bread is cooked. Cool on a wire rack and eat fresh.

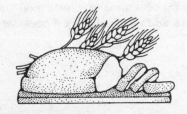

POTATO AND HORSERADISH PURÉE –
Kartoffelpüree Meerrettich

500 g POTATOES, COOKED UNTIL TENDER

2 TABLESPOONS BUTTER

3 TABLESPOONS SOUR CREAM

2 TABLESPOONS CHOPPED PARSLEY

PINCH VEGISALT

BLACK PEPPER

1 TABLESPOON HORSERADISH

Mash hot potatoes and add vegisalt and butter. Whip until light and creamy. Add remaining ingredients, mixing well, then pile into a serving dish. Serve hot.

RYE BREAD – *Roggenbrøt*

2 TABLESPOONS DRY ACTIVE YEAST

½ CUP TEPID WATER

2 TABLESPOONS BROWN SUGAR

½ CUP MOLASSES

3½ CUPS RYE FLOUR

1½ CUPS TEPID MILK

1 TEASPOON VEGISALT

2 TABLESPOONS BUTTER

2 CUPS WHOLEMEAL FLOUR

Dissolve yeast in water. Mix together milk, sugar and vegisalt. Beat in molasses, butter, yeast and water and 1 cup of rye flour. Gradually add remaining rye flour and enough of the wholemeal flour to make a stiff dough. Knead for 10 minutes or until pliable. Cover with a damp cloth and leave in a warm place for 1 hour to rise. Punch down and divide into 2 loaves. Allow to rise on a buttered baking sheet until double in size – this takes about 1½ hours. Bake in a preheated 375°F/190°C oven for 35 minutes or until brown.

APPLE BEGGAR – *Apfelbettelmann*

500g APPLES, PEELED AND SLICED

12 SLICES WHOLEMEAL BREAD, GRATED

1 TEASPOON CINNAMON

1 TABLESPOON ALMONDS, FINELY CHOPPED

1 TABLESPOON BUTTER

2 TABLESPOONS BROWN SUGAR

2 TABLESPOONS BUTTER

1 TEASPOON GRATED LEMON RIND

1 TABLESPOON RAISINS

Place apples and brown sugar in a pot with a little water. Simmer gently for 5 minutes. Cook bread in melted butter for 5 minutes. Stir in cinnamon, lemon rinds, almonds and raisins. Place half this mixture in a buttered pie dish. Add cooked apples, then top with remaining bread mixture. Dot with butter and bake in a hot (400°F/200°C) oven for 15-20 minutes or until golden brown. To serve, sprinkle with a little extra cinnamon and sugar and serve with yoghurt sweetened with a little Tia Maria and maple syrup. Delicious!

HAZELNUT OMELETTE – *Haselnussomeletten*

3 TABLESPOONS FLOUR

1 EGG, SEPARATED

2 TABLESPOONS GROUND HAZELNUTS

PINCH CINNAMON

1 CUP MILK

1 TABLESPOON BROWN SUGAR

2 TABLESPOONS BUTTER

Mix together flour, milk, egg yolk, sugar and hazelnuts. Beat egg white until stiff and fold into egg yolk mixture. Melt butter and fry omelette until golden brown. Turn and fry reverse side until brown then serve at once. To serve, dust with cinnamon and serve with fresh berries or stewed fruits.

OLD GERMAN MUFFINS – *Altdeutsche Brotchen*

200g BUTTER
2 EGGS
1 TEASPOON VANILLA ESSENCE
PINCH CINNAMON
250g WHOLEMEAL FLOUR
1 TABLESPOON GRATED ORANGE RIND
4 TABLESPOONS SUGAR
1 TABLESPOON RUM
3 TABLESPOONS MILK
1 TEASPOON BAKING POWDER
3 TABLESPOONS GROUND ALMONDS

Cream butter and sugar. Beat in eggs, rum, vanilla and milk. Mix together cinnamon, baking powder, flour, almonds and orange rind. Fold flour into butter mixture and half fill muffin or patty tins. Bake in a moderately hot (375°F/190°C) oven for 25 to 30 minutes until brown. These muffins do not store all that well, so eat fresh.

CHEESE TRUFFLES – *Käsetrüffel*

3 TABLESPOONS BUTTER
1 TEASPOON MILK
GRATED BLACK BREAD OR PUMPERNICKEL
125g CREAM CHEESE
1 TEASPOON HONEY

Cream butter and cream cheese. Beat in milk and honey and chill. Form into balls and roll in grated pumpernickel. Place 'truffles' on a serving dish and chill for at least 2 hours before serving.

SCANDINAVIA

Denmark ● Sweden ● Norway ● Finland

The food of Scandinavia is amongst the healthiest and heartiest in the world. High quality dairy produce and seafood feature with black rye and crispbreads, fresh vegetables, Arctic berries and, of course, the ubiquitous Danish pastry. Swedish meals are comfortable, relaxed and extremely healthy, with lots of salads and fresh fruits. Denmark is renowned for its aesthetic qualities and, in that country, meals look as good as they taste. Norway's hearty cuisine makes one aware of the cold climate and short days in that northernmost part of Europe where the locals rise at 5.00 am and go to bed by 9.00 pm. Finally, the food of Finland is remarkably similar to the cuisine of Russia. Bortsch, Blini, Paskha, Caviar, Salmon and Reindeer Tongue all make regular appearances on Finnish menus, and they are happily eaten and washed down with glasses of home-brewed mead and jigs of local vodka.

DENMARK

Danish days start off with Morgenmad, a simple breakfast consisting of rye bread, cheese and coffee. This is followed by open sandwiches, Smørrebrød, for lunch and perhaps a Danish pastry for afternoon tea. Dinner features fish or meat and vegetables which all seem to undergo long cooking processes – by our standards, at least – and a supper of cake, biscuits and warm milk may be taken later on in the evening.

Unsalted butter is used for all Danish cooking, although vegetable margarine makes a suitable substitute for those who can't eat butter.

DANISH CABBAGE WITH CARAWAY – *Røodkaal*

1 SMALL, FIRM RED CABBAGE, FINELY SHREDDED

3 TABLESPOONS SOYA OIL

1 TABLESPOON HONEY

125 ml RED WINE OR VEGETABLE STOCK

5 TABLESPOONS CIDER VINEGAR

2 TABLESPOONS TAMARI OR SOYA SAUCE

1 TEASPOON CARAWAY SEEDS

PINCH CAYENNE PEPPER

Cook cabbage in heated oil until soft. This takes 5-10 minutes over a low light, shaking the pan regularly to avoid catching. Gradually stir in honey, wine, vinegar, tamari, caraway seeds and pepper. Cover the pot, reduce to simmer and leave to cook over a very low light for about 2 1/2 hours. While the cabbage is cooking you will need to stir it from time to time and also add a little water as the liquid evaporates. The flavour of this cabbage is greatly improved if it is left for a day and then reheated and eaten the next.

DANISH OPEN SANDWICHES – *Smørrebrød*

Danish Smørrebrød *is the collective term used to describe a table of open sandwiches. In Denmark these appear in endless variety and beauty. It is important to garnish Smørrebrød with imagination and flair since their appearance is as important as their taste. Assemble the* Smørrebrød *using a combination of the ingredients listed below and serve with ice cold lager as they do in Denmark.*

Bases
Danish rye, black or firm wholemeal bread make the best bases for open sandwiches. Whatever bread you choose, it should be fairly substantial. Spread it with a layer of butter or vegetable margarine making sure you go right to the edges of the bread as this acts as a type of insulation.

Toppings
Cheese: *hard or soft cheese such as Camembert (with its rind) or creamy blue vein;* slices of hard-boiled egg moistened with a little mayonnaise; fish: *pickled, eg rollmops, smoked or fried;* cold meats: *grated vegetables, eg carrots.*

Garnishes
Vegetables: *slices of tomato, cucumber, radishes, onion rings, shallots;* herbs: *sprigs of parsley or watercress, chives;* seafood: *whole prawns, sardines, caviar;* sauces: *mayonnaise, tartar, horseradish, raw egg yolk;* fruit: *thinly sliced and twisted lemon or orange slices or lemon wedges, segments of mandarin, pitted cherries or prunes, fried bananas;* nuts: *all types chopped or whole, pickled walnuts;* meats: *crispy fried bacon etc.*

SUGAR-BROWN POTATOES – *Brunede Kartofler*

This is a very popular way of cooking potatoes in Denmark. It is made there with butter and sugar although it works quite well using the more natural ingredients suggested below.

8 kg NEW POTATOES
2 TABLESPOONS MAPLE SYRUP
2 TABLESPOONS VEGETABLE MARGARINE
1 TEASPOON TAMARI OR SOYA SAUCE

Wash and steam potatoes until tender. Remove skins if desired. Meanwhile, place maple syrup, vegetable margarine and tamari in a large frying pan or wok and heat gently. Add the potatoes, turning often so that they are completely coated in the syrup. When golden brown, remove from heat and serve immediately.

RHUBARB RELISH

Rhubarb is used in a savoury context here to make a ruby red relish which is served with roast chicken in the spring.

500g RHUBARB, CLEANED AND TRIMMED INTO SMALL PIECES
2 TABLESPOONS HONEY
2 TABLESPOONS WATER
1 TEASPOON CIDER VINEGAR

Combine all ingredients except vinegar in a pan. Place over a low light and simmer very slowly until the rhubarb is tender. Drain rhubarb, reserving cooking liquid. Pour syrup over rhubarb, stir in vinegar and set aside. When cool chill thoroughly before serving.

DANISH ONIONS

1 kg SMALL ONIONS
3 TABLESPOONS BUTTER OR VEGETABLE MARGARINE
6 TABLESPOONS DARK BROWN SUGAR
SPRIG FRESH ROSEMARY

Peel and steam onions until tender. Meanwhile, melt butter in a heavy pan. Add sugar and cook gently, stirring all the time. Add onions and continue to cook for a further 10 minutes or so. Add rosemary, cook for a few more minutes, and then serve. These onions are equally good hot or cold.

DANISH APPLE CAKE – *Aeblekage*

1 kg COOKING APPLES, PEELED AND THINLY SLICED

3 TABLESPOONS MAPLE SYRUP

100 g BUTTER OR VEGETABLE MARGARINE

2 CUPS BREADCRUMBS, MADE FROM FRESH WHOLEMEAL BREAD

2 TABLESPOONS BROWN SUGAR

125 ml YOGHURT

2 TABLESPOONS MILK

1 TABLESPOON MAPLE SYRUP

2 TABLESPOONS CHOPPED WALNUTS OR PECANS

Place apples in a pan with a little water and simmer gently until apples are well cooked. Remove from heat and beat thoroughly until the apples are smooth. Stir in maple syrup and leave to cool. Melt butter in a frying pan and stir in breadcrumbs. Cook over a medium heat until the crumbs are crisp and golden brown, then set aside. To assemble the 'cake' fill a glass serving bowl with alternate layers of apples and crumbs, making sure to begin and end with thin layers of crumbs. The layers of apple will be much thicker. Mix together yoghurt, milk and maple syrup and pile on top of the dessert. Sprinkle with chopped nuts, chill thoroughly and then serve.

NORWAY

The cold climate of Norway dictates the eating habits of that country where people enjoy a large breakfast at 5.00 or 6.00 am. Breakfast might include such delights as porridge, eggs, cheese, fish and meat as well as a variety of breads and crispbreads, butter and milk. Lunch at 11.00 am will often simply be an open sandwich while dinner is a more hearty affair. Dinner is a two to three course meal eaten at about 4.00 or 5.00 pm, and will often feature fish or game, accompanied by a variety of the 50 or 60 types of Norwegian bread that are available. Dairy produce and cold climate fruits such as berries and stone fruits are also eaten, both as appetisers and desserts.

POACHED SALMON, NORWEGIAN STYLE, WITH HORSERADISH SAUCE

1 LARGE ONION, SLICED
1 CUP CELERY TOPS, ROUGHLY CHOPPED
5 PEPPERCORNS
1 TEASPOON TAMARI OR SOYA SAUCE
1 kg SALMON FILLET
Horseradish Sauce
1 CUP YOGHURT
1 TEASPOON FRESHLY SQUEEZED LEMON JUICE
½ TEASPOON (OR MORE IF YOU LIKE IT HOT) HORSERADISH
SEA SALT AND FRESHLY GROUND BLACK PEPPER, TO TASTE
LEMON SLICES AND PARSLEY SPRIGS FOR GARNISH

Simmer onion, celery tops, peppercorns and soya sauce in about 2 litres boiling water for 30 minutes. Strain and then return to heat. Poach salmon gently in the broth until the fish flakes easily. This takes 10-15 minutes. Remove salmon from the broth and chill before serving. To make the sauce, combine yoghurt, lemon juice, horseradish, salt and pepper, mixing well. To serve, smother the salmon with the Horseradish Sauce and garnish with lemon slices and parsley.

LEMON CARROT SOUP

2 SMALL CARROTS, SLICED INTO JULIENNE (MATCHSTICK) STRIPS

5 VERY THIN SLICES LEMON

2 TEASPOONS FRESHLY SQUEEZED LEMON JUICE

SEA SALT AND FRESHLY GROUND BLACK PEPPER, TO TASTE

500 ml BEEF OR VEGETABLE STOCK

3 TABLESPOONS CHOPPED CHIVES

Place carrots, lemon slices, lemon juice, salt, pepper, stock and half the chives in a pan. Bring to the boil then simmer gently for 15 minutes. Serve immediately, making sure that each serving includes a slice of lemon. Garnish with the remaining chives.

CHERRY SOUP

1 kg PITTED CHERRIES

3 TABLESPOONS MAPLE SYRUP

3 SLICES LEMON

PINCH GROUND CINNAMON

PINCH ALLSPICE

3 TABLESPOONS SOUR CREAM

Place cherries, maple syrup, lemon slices, cinnamon and allspice in a pan. Barely cover with cold water and bring to the boil. Simmer gently for about 5 minutes then remove lemon slices. Bring back to the boil and then serve at once, garnished with a spoonful of sour cream.

ASPARAGUS WITH NUTMEG BUTTER

1 kg FRESH ASPARAGUS

6 TABLESPOONS BUTTER OR VEGETABLE MARGARINE

¼ TEASPOON GROUND NUTMEG

Trim asparagus spears and cook in a little rapidly boiling water for 5-10 minutes or until tender but still firm. Meanwhile, melt butter until it browns slightly. Stir in nutmeg and pour over drained asparagus. Serve immediately.

BEER BREAD – Øllebrød

This 'bread' is, in fact, a type of soup.

500 ml LAGER
250 ml WATER
1 TABLESPOON MAPLE SYRUP
2 EGG YOLKS
3 TABLESPOONS YOGHURT
4 TABLESPOONS CROÛTONS – SQUARES OF FRIED BREAD

Gently heat lager and water. Add maple syrup, egg yolks and yoghurt and continue to simmer slowly until the mixture just begins to boil, whisking all the time. Serve immediately with crispy croûtons.

NORWEGIAN FISHBALLS – *Fiskeboller*

500 g FISH TRIMMINGS
1 TABLESPOON VEGISALT
1.5 kg WHITE FISH FILLETS
75 g FINE BREADCRUMBS
2 EGGS
2 TABLESPOONS RICOTTA OR CREAM CHEESE
VEGISALT AND CAYENNE PEPPER, TO TASTE

Place fish trimmings and vegisalt in a large pan. Cover with water and simmer gently for 1 ½-2 hours. Meanwhile, mince fish by passing through a Mouli, mincer or food processor, but don't mince the fish too fine as it will become mushy that way. Place in a bowl and gradually work in breadcrumbs, beaten eggs and ricotta cheese. Season to taste and then refrigerate for 1 hour. Strain the fish trimmings, returning the stock to the pan. Shape the fish mixture into balls. Bring stock to boil and add fishballs, poaching gently for 10-15 minutes. Serve with mustard or horseradish.

SWEDEN

Swedish meals are relaxed and informal affairs – for the cook as well as everyone else – once he or she has done the preparations. When it is ready, the food is all placed on the table so that people can help themselves to the various courses as they wish. Desserts are simple and usually consist of fresh fruit and coffee although there are some exceptions, such as spiced fruits and sugary tarts.

SMORGASBORD

Smorgasbord in Sweden consists of a great variety of dishes. Traditionally, Smorgasbord was a huge table laden with cold meats, fish, eggs and salad, although these days it tends to be a little less elaborate than it was in the past. To prepare Smorgasbord, choose a selection of the following:

Cold fish: *pickled herrings, rollmops, smoked mackerel, trout, salmon, marinated fish, whole prawns, mussels, crayfish or crab with mayonnaise, roe or caviar;* **eggs:** *hard-boiled – sliced or stuffed;* **cold meats:** *chicken, turkey, ham, cold sausages, salami;* **salads:** *pickled beetroot or cucumbers, tomato and onion, Waldorf, green, crudites;* **pickles and relishes; breads:** *crispbreads, rye, wholemeal bread and butter;* **cheeses:** *hard, cream, ricotta and blue vein.*

GOTHENBURG COD

1 kg COD FILLETS (OR SIMILAR)

1 LARGE ONION, PEELED AND SLICED

PARSLEY AND LEMON WEDGES FOR GARNISH

2 TEASPOONS VEGISALT

Place fish in a large frying pan with onion slices and some of the parsley and vegisalt. Barely cover with water, bring to the boil then reduce heat to simmer for 15-20 minutes. Remove fish from pan, garnish with lemon wedges and remaining parsley and serve immediately with steamed potatoes and a crisp salad.

HERRING SALAD – *Sillsallad*

3-4 ROLLMOP HERRINGS

3 SMALL POTATOES, COOKED AND PEELED

3 SMALL BEETROOT, COOKED AND PEELED

1 SMALL APPLE, FINELY CHOPPED

1 PICKLED CUCUMBER, FINELY CHOPPED

1 STICK CELERY, FINELY CHOPPED

Dressing

3 TABLESPOONS BROWN RICE OR CIDER VINEGAR

1 TABLESPOON WATER

1 TEASPOON HONEY

1 TEASPOON TAMARI OR SOYA SAUCE

Garnish

2 EGGS, HARD-BOILED AND SLICED

125 ml SOUR CREAM OR THICK YOGHURT

SPRIG FRESH DILL

Soak herring overnight in cold water. Next day, drain herring and chop finely. Place in a bowl with diced potatoes, beetroot, apple, cucumber and celery. Place dressing ingredients in a glass jar, screw the lid on tightly and shake well. Stir dressing gently into herring mixture and refrigerate for a few hours. To serve, garnish with egg slices, sour cream or yoghurt and dill.

WEST COAST SALAD – *Vastkustsallad*

This seafood salad originates from Sweden's west coast where the best catches are made.

500g PEELED PRAWNS

500g PEELED LOBSTER, CRAYFISH OR CRABMEAT

250g COOKED PEAS

250g TOMATOES, SKINNED AND CHOPPED

1 SMALL CUCUMBER, PEELED AND SLICED

125g MUNG BEAN OR ALFALFA SPROUTS

Dressing

3 TABLESPOONS COLD PRESSED SALAD OIL

2 TABLESPOONS WHITE WINE VINEGAR

1 CLOVE GARLIC, CRUSHED

1 TABLESPOON FRESH DILL, FINELY CHOPPED

Garnish

A FEW CRISP LETTUCE LEAVES

SOYA MAYONNAISE

FRESH DILL

Place all salad ingredients in a bowl. Mix dressing ingredients together well and drizzle over fish. Stir gently, cover and refrigerate 1-2 hours. To serve, pile salad onto lettuce leaves, top with mayonnaise and garnish with dill.

JANSSON'S TEMPTATION – *Jansson's Frestelse*

2 LARGE ONIONS, CHOPPED

2 TABLESPOONS UNSALTED BUTTER

4 POTATOES, THINLY SLICED

1 SMALL CAN ANCHOVIES

SEA SALT AND FRESHLY GROUND BLACK PEPPER, TO TASTE

1 CUP MILK

2 TABLESPOONS BREADCRUMBS

Sauté onion in butter till soft. Place layers of potatoes, onion and anchovies in a buttered casserole dish, ending with a layer of potatoes and seasoning each layer to taste. Pour milk over casserole and top with breadcrumbs. Bake in a moderate oven (180°C, 350°F, Gas 4) for about 1 hour or until the potatoes are cooked and the top of the dish is golden brown and crunchy.

STOCKLHOLM BROWN BEANS

500g BROWN BEANS, SOAKED OVERNIGHT

1 LITRE WATER

SEA SALT AND FRESHLY GROUND BLACK PEPPER, TO TASTE

2 TEASPOONS TAMARI OR SOYA SAUCE

3 TABLESPOONS BROWN RICE OR WINE VINEGAR

3 TABLESPOONS MAPLE SYRUP

Simmer beans in soaking water for 2-3 hours or until the beans are soft but not mushy. Add salt during the cooking process. When tender, add tamari, vinegar and maple syrup, stirring well. Cook one hour longer, adding a little water if and when necessary. Season with black pepper and a little extra maple syrup or vinegar if desired. Traditionally served with sour cream, these beans are also good with yoghurt.

FINLAND

Suomi, the Finnish name for Finland, brings to mind impressions of snow and saunas, fjords and frosts, Laplanders and endless beautiful lakes fringed with conifers and filled with fish. The Finnish diet consists largely of dairy products, seafood and all types of berries in season – such as cranberries, cloudberries and rare Arctic brambles. The following recipes are a mere taste of the vast and varied cuisine of Finland.

SOUP SUOMI – *Kalakeitto*

A type of Finnish fish soup.

1 kg POTATOES, THICKLY SLICED

2 ONIONS, SLICED

2 LITRES WATER

1 kg FISH FILLETS, eg TROUT, PERCH, BREAM

PINCH ALLSPICE

PINCH SEA SALT

1 THICK SLICE BUTTERED RYE BREAD

2 TABLESPOONS WHOLEMEAL FLOUR

CRAM OR YOGHURT

FRESH DILL FOR GARNISH

Simmer the potatoes and onions in gently boiling water for about 10 minutes. Add fish fillets, allspice, salt and rye bread, cover and simmer for a further 15 minutes. Remove fish from pan with a slotted spoon and keep warm. Add a little of the fish stock to the flour to form a paste. Return the paste to the pot and stir well over a medium heat to thicken the soup. Put the fish back into the pot, simmer for a few more minutes and add a little extra salt if desired. Serve hot, garnished with a swirl of cream or yoghurt and some fresh dill.

BEETROOT SOUP – *Bortsch*

250 g CARROTS, SLICED
½ SMALL HEAD CABBAGE, SHREDDED
500 g TOMATOES, SKINNED AND CHOPPED
1 LITRE VEGETABLE STOCK
500 g BEETROOT, COOKED AND SLICED
PINCH CAYENNE PEPPER
1 TEASPOON TAMARI OR SOYA SAUCE
1 TABLESPOON CIDER VINEGAR
4 TABLESPOONS YOGHURT
½ TEASPOON CARAWAY SEEDS

Place carrots, cabbage, tomatoes and stock in a pot. Bring to the boil, then reduce to simmer for 30 minutes. Chop or grate beetroot and add to soup. Stir in cayenne and tamari and simmer for a further 15-20 minutes. Stir in vinegar, cover and leave for 5 minutes off the heat. Serve garnished with yoghurt and a few caraway seeds.

CUCUMBER SALAD – *Salaattia*

2 CUCUMBERS, PEELED
SEA SALT AND BROWN SUGAR
3-4 TABLESPOONS WINE VINEGAR
FRESH DILL

Slice the cucumbers with a potato peeler to make super thin slices. This is a very laborious task but well worth while. You could start off with just one cucumber if you find the slicing too tedious. Alternatively, use the thinnest slicing blade of a food processor to obtain the ultra paper-thin slices of cucumber needed for this salad. When peeled, sprinkle with salt and sugar and leave for 30 minutes. Drain away liquid and then place in a shallow dish. Toss in vinegar and chill for a few hours before serving. To serve, garnish with fresh dill.

BUCKWHEAT PANCAKES – *Blini*

These buckwheat yeasted pancakes came to Finland from Russia and are traditionally served with cold accompaniments such as hard-boiled eggs, onion slices, sour cream and pickled cucumbers.

1 TABLESPOON HONEY
125 ml TEPID WATER
1 TABLESPOON DRIED YEAST
125 ml MILK
1 TABLESPOON BUTTER
125 g WHOLEMEAL FLOUR
125 g BUCKWHEAT FLOUR
PINCH VEGISALT
1 EGG, SEPARATED
3 TABLESPOONS MINERAL WATER

Dissolve honey in tepid water. Sprinkle in yeast and leave in a warm place until mixture becomes frothy – this takes 10-15 minutes. heat milk and butter slowly but do not allow to boil. Sift flours, add vegisalt, yeast water, egg yolk and mineral water. Stir well until mixture becomes smooth then put aside in a warm place to rise – this takes 1-2 hours. When mixture has doubled in size, gently fold in stiffly beaten egg white. To cook, heat a little oil, spread batter into pan and cook over a medium heat until golden brown. Slip over and repeat on the other side. Serve with accompaniments such as hard-boiled eggs, rollmops, caviar, sour cream, smoked fish, lemon juice, pickled cucumbers and raw onions.

HELSINKI MUSHROOMS – *Säilötyt Sienet*

500 g BUTTON MUSHROOMS
WINE VINEGAR
3 TABLESPOONS HONEY
MUSLIN BAG CONTAINING SPICES: 1 STICK CINNAMON, 1 SMALL SLICE FRESH GINGER, A FEW CLOVES, A FEW PEPPERCORNS

Wash mushrooms and slice finely. Place in a glass jar and cover with vinegar. Leave overnight. Next day, strain vinegar into a pan. Add honey and spice bag and bring to the boil. Simmer for 15 minutes and then pour over mushrooms. Repeat this process every day for three days, finally discarding spice bag. Serve these spicy vinegared mushrooms as a smorgasbord dish or with seafood.

FINNISH POTATO PUDDING – *Imellytetty Perunavuoka*

1 kg POTATOES

2 TABLESPOONS WHEATGERM

1 TABLESPOON MAPLE SYRUP

1 TEASPOON TAMARI OR SOYA SAUCE

500 ml MILK

1 TABLESPOON BUTTER

1 TABLESPOON BREADCRUMBS

Boil potatoes until cooked and then peel. Mash while still hot then stir in wheatgerm and maple syrup. Set aside in a cool place for a few hours, stirring occasionally. Mix in tamari, milk and butter then place in a buttered casserole dish. Top with breadcrumbs and bake in a moderate oven (180°C/Gas 4/350°F) for one hour. This pudding is traditionally served as a savoury dish with the Sunday roast.

RUSSIA

My grandmother was Russian and I still treasure childhood memories of her noodles! She used to make a large quantity of egg dough, roll it out thinly and hang sections of it on the clothes line to dry in the sun. When they were almost dry, she'd take the floury sheets down, cut them into strips and then leave them to dry out completely before putting them away for later use. Over the following weeks, out came the noodles in various guises: boiled and served with a ricotta-type cream cheese and perhaps some pickled cucumbers, floated in the ubiquitous dish of chicken soup or sometimes, as a winter treat, they would appear dripping in honey and smothered in nuts for an unusual and very special dessert.

It's this sort of food that has given Russian cooking a bad reputation. It is known for heavy, stodgy food and clearly the dumplings and cabbage rolls, black bread, borscht and sour cream are solid, dour foods designed to stave off the bitter cold. However, the Soviet Union covers an enormous area and its cuisine is similarly vast and varied, as the following regional recipes attempt to show. Try some of them and I'm sure you'll be pleasantly surprised. The use of fresh fruits, vegetables and tasty, cold water fish accompanied by Kasha *(buckwheat),* Pilau *(rice) or* Lapsha *(noodles) and garnished with* Smeyetana *(sour cream) and dill, make for a rich, but very healthy and delicious diet.*

SORREL SOUP – *Sup Shchavyeliemi*

This soup can be made with spinach or silverbeet if sorrel is not available.

5 MEDIUM-SIZED POTATOES
1.5 litres CHICKEN OR VEGETABLE STOCK
1 LARGE BUNCH SORREL
1 EGG YOLK
1 TABLESPOON BUTTER
1 TABLESPOON TAMARI OR SOYA SAUCE
PINCH CAYENNE PEPPER
PAPRIKA TO GARNISH

Scrub potatoes and simmer in stock until soft. Rub through a sieve or blend in a food processor and set aside. Wash the sorrel thoroughly and then cook in a pot without adding any extra water. Stir from time to time until sorrel is soft and then add to the potato purée and stock and simmer 20-30 minutes. Just before serving, beat the egg yolk with the butter and gently stir this mixture into the soup. Season to taste with tamari and cayenne, garnish with paprika and serve hot.

FRESH FRUIT SOUP – *Sup Iz Svyezhiki Fruktov*

500g GREEN COOKING APPLES, PEELED AND DICED
500g PEARS, PEELED AND DICED
500ml WATER
2 TABLESPOONS HONEY
1 TABLESPOON POTATO FLOUR (OR CORNFLOUR)
A FEW SLICES LEMON
SOUR CREAM

Simmer apples and pears in boiling water until soft. Stir in honey then rub through a sieve or process in a blender. Return to the pan and bring back to the boil then reduce to simmer. Meanwhile, make a paste out of the potato flour with a little cold water then stir this into the soup and simmer for 5 minutes. Add lemon slices and serve hot or cold, with a spoonful of sour cream.

UKRANIAN BORSCHT – *Borscht Ukrainski*

1.5 litres CHICKEN OR VEGETABLE STOCK

2 TABLESPOONS APPLE CIDER VINEGAR

250 g BEETROOT, FINELY DICED

2 LARGE POTATOES, SCRUBBED AND DICED

¼ SMALL, FIRM CABBAGE, FINELY SHREDDED

2 LARGE TOMATOES, SKINNED AND CHOPPED

1 SMALL ONION, VERY FINELY CHOPPED

1 BAY LEAF

A FEW CARAWAY SEEDS

GOOD PINCH VEGISALT

FRESHLY GROUND BLACK PEPPER

SOUR CREAM TO GARNISH

Bring stock and vinegar to the boil, then add beetroot and cook until almost soft. Add potatoes and continue cooking for 10 minutes, then add cabbage, tomatoes and onion. Simmer gently for 10-15 minutes and then add bay leaf, caraway seeds, vegisalt and plenty of black pepper, and continue cooking 15 minutes longer. Serve hot or cold, garnished with a good spoonful of sour cream.

BEANS AND SOUR CREAM – *Fasoli Smyetana*

500 g GREEN BEANS, TOPPED, TAILED AND SLICED

1 TABLESPOON BUTTER

PINCH VEGISALT

FRESHLY GROUND BLACK PEPPER

125 ml SOUR CREAM

2 HARD BOILED EGGS, ROUGHLY CHOPPED

2 TABLESPOONS DILL, CHOPPED

Boil or steam beans until tender but still crunchy. Heat butter in pan and return drained beans. Cook for a couple of minutes, then add salt, pepper and sour cream. Heat through and serve garnished with egg and dill.

PICKLED MUSHROOMS – *Marinovanye Griby*

Small, white mushrooms are the best ones to use for this recipe.

500g BUTTON MUSHROOMS, WASHED THOROUGHLY
125ml WATER
125ml WHITE WINE VINEGAR
1 HEAPED TEASPOON COARSE SEA-SALT
1 TEASPOON PEPPERCORNS
2 BAY LEAVES

Simmer mushrooms, whole or sliced, in the boiling water, vinegar and salt for just a few minutes. Drain, reserving the liquid and pack the mushrooms into sterilised glass jars. Return the vinegar marinade to the pot and bring to the boil. Add peppercorns and bay leaves and simmer for 10-15 minutes, or until the mixture has reduced in quantity significantly. Strain and allow to cool. Pour marinade over mushrooms, seal tightly and leave for several days before using. If you like, you can add whole cloves of garlic or slices of onion to the marinade.

BEETROOTS AND DILL – *Svyekla B Ukropomi*

4 MEDIUM-SIZED BEETROOTS
1 TABLESPOON BUTTER
1 ONION, FINELY CHOPPED
PINCH VEGISALT
PINCH CAYENNE PEPPER
½ TEASPOON HONEY
1 TEASPOON MISO
125ml SOUR CREAM OR YOGHURT
2 TABLESPOONS DILL, CHOPPED

Boil beetroots until tender. Allow to cool for 10 minutes or so, and then peel and dice. Heat butter and sauté onion for 5 minutes. Add beetroot, salt, cayenne and honey and continue to cook over a low heat for 5-10 minutes. Just before serving, stir in miso and when it is dissolved, add sour cream. Heat through then serve garnished with dill.

CABBAGE AND TOMATO – *Kapusti I Pomidory*

3 TABLESPOONS BUTTER

2 ONIONS, VERY FINELY SLICED

2 CLOVES GARLIC, FINELY CHOPPED

4 SMALL FIRM WHITE CABBAGE, FINELY SHREDDED

3 TOMATOES, SKINNED AND CHOPPED

2 TEASPOONS HONEY

2 TEASPOONS TAMARI OR SOYA SAUCE

FRESHLY GROUND BLACK PEPPER

3 TABLESPOONS FINELY CHOPPED PARSLEY

Heat butter and gently sauté onion and garlic for 5 minutes. Add cabbage, stir well and continue to cook 5 minutes longer. Stir in tomatoes, honey, tamari and pepper, cover and simmer for 15 minutes. Serve hot, garnished with parsley.

HERRING PIE – *Forshmak Iz Seldi*

2 SALTED HERRINGS, SOAKED IN MILK OVERNIGHT

4 SLICES WHOLEMEAL BREAD, CRUSTS REMOVED

125 ml MILK

5 MEDIUM-SIZED POTATOES, SCRUBBED AND DICED

2 CRISP GREEN APPLES, PEELED AND DICED

2 MEDIUM-SIZED ONIONS, VERY FINELY CHOPPED

FRESHLY GROUND BLACK PEPPER

PINCH VEGISALT

2 TABLESPOONS DILL, FINELY CHOPPED

3 TABLESPOONS PARSLEY, FINELY CHOPPED

125 ml SOUR CREAM OR YOGHURT

2 EGGS, LIGHTLY BEATEN

3 TABLESPOONS WHEAT GERM

Remove skin and bones from fish after it has been left to soak overnight. Chop fish and set aside. Soak bread in milk and leave 10 minutes or so, then squeeze out excess moisture. Mix together all remaining ingredients, including fish but excluding wheat germ until thoroughly combined. Pile into a buttered pie dish, sprinkle with wheat germ and bake in a moderate oven for 30 minutes or until golden brown.

PERCH WITH SOUR CREAM – *Morsky Pod Smyetana*

1 kg PERCH FILLETS

3 TABLESPOONS FLOUR

PINCH VEGISALT

3 TABLESPOONS LIGHT COOKING OIL

1 TABLESPOON FLOUR

125 ml FISH OR VEGETABLE STOCK

250 ml SOUR CREAM

5-6 SHALLOTS, DIAGONALLY SLICED

3 HARD-BOILED EGGS, CHOPPED

3 TABLESPOONS PARSLEY, FINELY CHOPPED

Wash fish fillets and pat dry. Combine flour with salt and then dust fish with this mixture. Cook fish lightly in hot oil until golden brown on both sides then remove to a buttered pan and keep hot. Stir an extra tablespoon of flour into the pan in which the fish has been cooked and then gradually stir in stock to make a sauce. When well mixed, stir in sour cream and simmer over a very low light for a few minutes. Pour sauce over fish and bake in a moderate oven for 10-15 minutes. Garnish with shallots, eggs and parsley and serve hot with potatoes, mushrooms and a green salad.

BUCKWHEAT BREAM – *Lyesch Farishrovanyi Kashya*

125 g HULLED BUCKWHEAT

1 SMALL ONION, VERY FINELY CHOPPED

1 TEASPOON TAMARI OR SOYA SAUCE

2 TEASPOONS OLIVE OIL

2 TABLESPOONS DILL, FINELY CHOPPED

4 WHOLE BREAM, CLEANED AND GUTTED

200 ml SOUR CREAM OR YOGHURT

3 TABLESPOONS BREADCRUMBS

3 TABLESPOONS WHEAT GERM

Place the buckwheat in a pot and cover with water (about 1½ times the amount of water). Stir in onion and tamari and bring to the boil. Reduce to simmer, cover and cook until tender – approximately 25 minutes – or until all the water is evaporated and the grains are separate but not soggy. Stir in the olive oil and dill and place in a warm oven for 10 minutes to dry out. Use this mixture to stuff the fish. Place stuffed fish in a buttered baking dish, top with sour cream, breadcrumbs and wheat germ, and bake in a moderate oven 25-30 minutes. It helps to baste the fish occasionally during the cooking process. Serve hot, garnished with a little extra dill.

CHICKEN WITH APPLES – *Tsyplyenok S Yablokami*

1 FREE-RANGE CHICKEN, CUT INTO SERVING PIECES

3 TABLESPOONS WHOLEMEAL FLOUR

1 TABLESPOON VEGISALT

3 TABLESPOONS BUTTER

2 TABLESPOONS LIGHT COOKING OIL

4-5 MEDIUM SIZED CRISP, GREEN APPLES, PEELED AND SLICED

250 ml CHICKEN OR VEGETABLE STOCK

125 ml WHITE WINE

FRESHLY GROUND BLACK PEPPER

1 TEASPOON TARRAGON

Lightly coat chicken pieces with flour and vegisalt. Heat butter and oil and then brown the chicken pieces for 4-5 minutes per side or until golden. Place the chicken in a casserole dish and cover with apples, stock and wine. Place in a moderate (350°F/180°C) oven and cook for 40-45 minutes, or until chicken is tender and sauce has thickened. Serve with hot rice and salad.

FISH CAKES – *Bitki Iz Ryby*

500g FIRM WHITE FISH FILLETS, FINELY CHOPPED
2 SLICES WHOLEMEAL BREAD
3-4 TABLESPOONS MILK
1 TEASPOON VEGISALT
FRESHLY GROUND BLACK PEPPER
2 EGGS, WELL BEATEN
BREADCRUMBS
125g MUSHROOMS, FINELY SLICED
200ml FISH OR VEGETABLE STOCK

Mix fish with bread soaked in milk. Season with salt and pepper and put through a mincer or food processor. Bind together with half the beaten egg and then shape into cakes or patties. Dip in egg and coat with breadcrumbs, then place in a baking dish. Place mushroom slices in amongst the fish cakes and then pour in stock. Cover and bake in a moderate oven for 30 minutes. Serve hot with buckwheat or rice and salad.

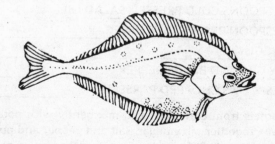

BEETROOT SALAD – *Salat Iz Svyekli*

6 MEDIUM-SIZED BEETROOTS

3 TABLESPOONS APPLE CIDER VINEGAR

2 TABLESPOONS COLD PRESSED SALAD OIL

1 TABLESPOON ORANGE JUICE

PINCH VEGISALT

PINCH CAYENNE PEPPER

A FEW CARAWAY SEEDS

PINCH DRIED CLOVES

PINCH DRIED CINNAMON

½ TEASPOON LEMON PEEL, VERY FINELY GRATED

½ TEASPOON ORANGE PEEL, VERY FINELY GRATED

Bake beetroots in a moderate oven for one hour or until soft. Peel and slice finely, then place in a shallow serving bowl. Mix together vinegar, oil, orange juice, vegisalt, cayenne, caraway seeds, cloves, cinnamon and peel. Pour dressing over beetroot and allow to cool before serving. To serve, garnish with a little very finely sliced orange or lemon peel.

CORN AND POTATO SALAD – *Salat Is Kartofyelya I Kukuruzi*

3 COBS CORN, COOKED UNTIL TENDER

4 MEDIUM-SIZED POTATOES, DICED AND COOKED TILL TENDER

3 TABLESPOONS CHIVES, FINELY CHOPPED

2 TABLESPOONS COLD PRESSED SALAD OIL

1 TABLESPOON BROWN RICE VINEGAR

PINCH VEGISALT

FRESHLY GROUND BLACK PEPPER

2 TABLESPOONS CHOPPED PARSLEY

Scrap kernels from corn cobs and mix gently with potato and chives. Mix together oil, vinegar, salt and pepper and pour over corn and potato. Chill for at least an hour then serve garnished with chopped parsley.

BLACK RUSSIAN APPLE CHARLOTTE – *Babka Yablochnia*

1 kg GREEN APPLES, PEELED AND CHOPPED
2 TABLESPOONS HONEY
250 kg BLACK BREADCRUMBS, MADE FROM STALE PUMPERNICKEL OR BLACK RYE BREAD
3 TABLESPOONS GOOD QUALITY OIL
2 EGGS, SEPARATED
1 GLASS SWEET WHITE WINE
125 g BLACK SULTANAS
2 TABLESPOONS BLANCHED ALMONDS, FINELY CHOPPED
1 TEASPOON ORANGE PEEL, VERY FINELY GRATED
1 TEASPOON LEMON PEEL, VERY FINELY GRATED
2-3 CLOVES
PINCH NUTMEG
PINCH CINNAMON
PINCH ALLSPICE

Place apples and honey in a pot with a little water and cook till almost soft. Add breadcrumbs and oil and set aside. Beat egg yolks until thick and creamy then stir in remaining ingredients, including apple mixture. Beat egg whites until stiff, then fold into apple mixture. Heap into a buttered pie or soufflé dish and bake in a moderate oven for 45-50 minutes. Serve with sour cream or yoghurt and a sweetened apricot sauce (below).

APRICOT SAUCE – *Sous Iz Kuragi*

250 g DRIED APRICOTS
3 TABLESPOONS HONEY

Wash apricots then place in a pan. Cover with water and leave overnight. Next day, bring to boil then reduce to simmer until fruit is cooked. Rub through a sieve or blend in a food processor, and return to the pan. Stir in honey and continue to cook over a very low heat for 5-10 minutes.

BABY PANCAKES – *Blinchiki*

Blinchiki or 'Baby Blini' are small pancakes which are stuffed with sweetened cream cheese and raisins, stewed fruit or minced meat and refried. They can, alternatively, be served hot with sour cream and fruit sauce such as the apricot sauce above.

2 EGGS, SEPARATED
PINCH SALT
1 TEASPOON SUGAR
500 ml MILK
250 ml WHOLEMEAL FLOUR, SIFTED
BUTTER FOR FRYING

Beat egg yolks, salt and sugar till thick and creamy. Gradually beat in milk and then stir in flour. Beat until the mixture is smooth and leave for 30 minutes to settle. This mixture can also be made in a food processor or blender, in which case it is not necessary to 'rest' it before using. To cook 'blinchiki' heat a little butter in a small, heavy pan. When hot, drop in a tablespoonful of batter and cook until golden brown on one side only. Remove from pan with a spatula, dust with a little flour and then return to the pan to cook the other side. Stack the pancakes in a pile and wrap in a cloth to keep warm.

HONEY MOUSSE – *Myedovyi Muss*

1 CUP HONEY
4 EGGS, SEPARATED

Beat egg yolks and stir in honey. Place in a double boiler and cook over boiling water, stirring all the while until the egg and honey mixture thickens. Remove from heat and set aside to cool. Beat egg whites until stiff peaks form and fold into egg yolks. Spoon into individual dishes or champagne glasses and allow to chill before serving.

SWEET WALNUT OMELETTE – *Yaichnitsa S Oryekhami*

2 TABLESPOONS CHOPPED WALNUTS

1 TABLESPOON BUTTER

2 TABLESPOONS WHOLEMEAL BREADCRUMBS

2 TABLESPOONS HONEY

4 EGGS, LIGHTLY BEATEN

2 TABLESPOONS MILK OR CREAM

LEMON JUICE

Sauté walnuts in butter for a few minutes. Stir in breadcrumbs and continue to cook for 2-3 minutes then stir in 1 tablespoon of honey. Remove the pan from the heat and gently pour in the eggs and cream. Return to the stove and cook as an ordinary omelette. Flip over and cook the other side and serve hot, sprinkled generously with freshly squeezed lemon juice and the extra honey if desired.

APPLE SOUFFLÉ – *Vozdushnyi Pirog Iz Yablock*

4 LARGE OR 6 MEDIUM-SIZED COOKING APPLES

4 EGG WHITES, STIFFLY BEATEN

2 TABLESPOONS SUGAR

Place the apples on a buttered baking dish and bake in a hot oven until soft – this takes anything from 35-50 minutes according to the size of the apples. When soft, peel the apples and rub through a sieve. Stir in sugar and then cook apple purée over a low light, stirring constantly until it thickens. Fold in the egg whites, while the apple purée is still hot, then pile into a soufflé dish. Bake in a moderate (350°F/180°C) oven for 25-30 minutes or until golden brown. Serve at once with sour cream or thick yoghurt sweetened with a little honey.

THE MIDDLE EAST

Lebanon • Jordan • Egypt • Kuwait • Syria •
Yemen • Oman • Armenia • Iraq • Iran • Saudi Arabia

The Arabian states have provided the world with exotic ingredients and dishes quite beyond those that are suspended in daily limbo behind the heated glass walls of Lebanese take-away shops. The opulence of the Middle East is exemplified in simple dishes containing oranges, avocados, dates and pistachio nuts – dishes which are light enough to enjoy on balmy summer nights or on blazing hot days.

Hailing from troubled Lebanon, Syria, Jordan, neighbouring Israel and Iraq, Saudi Arabia and the oil rich states of the Arabian Gulf, the cuisine of the Middle East cuts across national frontiers and is surprisingly similar throughout the region. At once both rich and thrifty, Arabian dishes made with natural ingredients are healthful, tasty and simple to prepare.

Entrees

Humus and Tahini • Lentil and Spinach Soup

Yoghurt Cheese Balls • Hilbeh – *Fenugreek Paste*

Pickled Turnips • Stuffed Onions

Carrot and Chickpea Soup • Melokhia – *Arabian Mallow Soup*

Pitta Bread •Hot Carrot Pickle

Salads

Chickpea Salad • Shallot and Radish Salad •
Tomato and Coriander Salad

Main Course

Vegetable Kibbeh • Stuffed Eggplant • Sesame Fish
Green Beans in Oil • Saffron Rice • Paprika Fish Casserole

Desserts

Baked Rice Pudding • Tahini Custard • Date Rolls
Arabic Yoghurt Cake • Halvah • Lassia – *Yoghurt Drink*

HUMUS AND TAHINI (Lebanon)

100 g CHICKPEAS

2 LEMONS, JUICED

2 CLOVES GARLIC, CRUSHED

3 TABLESPOONS TAHINI

SEA SALT AND BLACK PEPPER, TO TASTE

1 TABLESPOON OLIVE OIL

PINCH CAYENNE PEPPER

CHOPPED PARSLEY

Soak chickpeas overnight. The following day simmer for 2 hours, reserving the cooking water. Blend together chickpeas, lemon juice, garlic, tahini and cooking water as required. Use a food processor or blender for this job, adding cooking water and oil if necessary. When well blended, season to taste with salt and pepper. Serve garnished with oil, cayenne and chopped parsley.

LENTIL AND SPINACH SOUP – *Adas Bis Silq (Lebanon)*

1½ CUPS BROWN LENTILS

1 LITRE WATER

SMALL BUNCH SPINACH

3 TABLESPOONS OLIVE OIL

2 ONIONS, FINELY CHOPPED

3 CLOVES GARLIC, CRUSHED

3 TABLESPOONS FINELY CHOPPED PARSLEY

SEA SALT AND FRESHLY GROUND BLACK PEPPER, TO TASTE

2 TABLESPOONS FRESHLY SQUEEZED LEMON JUICE

Place lentils in pot with cold water. Bring to boil then reduce to simmer 1 hour until lentils are soft. It may be necessary to skim the foam from the top of the pot occasionally. While the lentils are cooking, prepare the spinach by washing well and shredding roughly. Heat the oil and fry the onions and garlic till soft. Add the spinach and cook over medium heat until it wilts. Add spinach and onions to the cooked lentils, stir in parsley, seasoning and lemon juice and simmer 20 minutes. Serve hot with pitta bread.

YOGHURT CHEESE BALLS – *Labneh Makbus (Syria)*

500g NATURAL YOGHURT

SALT

CHEESECLOTH OR MUSLIN

OLIVE OIL

Place yoghurt in the centre of the cheesecloth, sprinkle with salt and then tie up and leave suspended over a bowl so that the whey can drip freely. This usually takes 12 hours or so. When drained, take a teaspoonful at a time and form into balls. Refrigerate the yoghurt balls for several hours until they are firm, then pack into a sterilised glass jar. Cover with olive oil, seal and store. These cheese balls make a good snack if served with pitta bread and some of the olive oil they are stored in.

FENUGREEK PASTE – *Hilbeh (Yemen)*

1 TABLESPOON FENUGREEK SEEDS
½ CUP COLD WATER
3 CLOVES GARLIC
1 BUNCH FRESH CORIANDER, FINELY CHOPPED
SEA SALT, TO TASTE
2 TEASPOONS LEMON JUICE
¼ TEASPOON CHILLI POWDER
1 TABLESPOON FINELY CHOPPED ONION

Soak fenugreek seeds in cold water overnight. They are quite mucilaginous, so don't think there is anything wrong with them – the gel is natural. Drain seeds and place in food processor or blender with remaining ingredients, using a little cold water if necessary, to mix. This operation can, of course, be carried out using a mortar and pestle if preferred. When well mixed, pour Hilbeh into a jar and refrigerate. Use as a dip, with pitta bread or as a relish.

PICKLED TURNIPS – *Achar Lefet (Oman)*

1 kg BABY WHITE TURNIPS
1 SMALL BEETROOT, PEELED AND SLICED
1 CLOVE GARLIC
500 ml WHITE WINE VINEGAR
2 CUPS WATER
1 TEASPOON FENNEL SEEDS
1 TABLESPOON SALT

Peel the turnips and cut into halves or quarters and pack, together with the beetroot, into sterilised jars. Place slices of garlic between the layers. Bring vinegar to the boil with 2 cups water, the fennel seeds and salt, the pour immediately over the vegetables. Seal tightly and leave for at least 2 weeks before using. Once opened, the pickles should be refrigerated.

STUFFED ONIONS – *Mahasha (Kuwait)*

This dish can be served hot or cold, on its own or as an accompaniment to a main course.

6 LARGE ONIONS

3 TABLESPOONS OLIVE OIL

Stuffing
100g LONG GRAIN BROWN RICE

100g SOYA GRITS

1 LEMON

3 TOMATOES, SKINNED AND CHOPPED

1 TABLESPOON PARSLEY, FINELY CHOPPED

1 TEASPOON TURMERIC

PINCH CARDAMOM

SEA SALT AND FRESHLY GROUND BLACK PEPPER, TO TASTE

Simmer the unpeeled onions in a pot of water for about 20 minutes. Drain and cool before peeling. Carefully dismantle the onion, layer by layer and then stuff with small ovals of the following mixture.

Stuffing – Wash the rice and then place in a pot with the soya grits, juice and rind of lemon, tomatoes, parsley, turmeric, cardamom, salt and pepper

To cook, place the stuffed onions in a pan of sizzling oil. Brown for 5 minutes per side then place in a large cooking pot. Simmer in a mixture of stock, water and/or reserved juices for 45-50 minutes or until the rice is cooked and the liquid has evaporated. You may need to uncover the pot for the last 10 minutes or so.

PITTA BREAD

1 TEASPOON HONEY

1-2 CUPS WARM WATER

1 TABLESPOON DRY ACTIVE YEAST

1 TEASPOON SALT

1 TABLESPOON OLIVE OIL

500g WHOLEMEAL FLOUR

Mix together honey and water. Sprinkle yeast into this mixture and leave to stand in a warm place for 5 minutes or until frothy. Stir in salt, oil and about 2 cups of the flour. Knead dough on a floured surface, using more flour to prevent sticking, for about 5-10 minutes. When smooth and elastic, place dough in a bowl and leave to rise in a warm place for at least 2 hours, although you can leave it up to 10 hours if you wish. Punch down dough and divide into 8 pieces. Roll each into a circular or oval shape about 5 cm (¼ inch) thick. Place on oiled baking sheets and set in a warm place for half an hour. Meanwhile, preheat oven to 475°F (240°C/ Gas 9) and bake the pitta bread for about 10 minutes. They are ready when puffed – their colour does not change significantly. Wrap in a cloth to keep soft. Serve hot or at room temperature. These breads can be stored in a freezer if required.

ARABIAN MALLOW SOUP – *Melokhia (Egypt)*

Mallow can be found growing wild around the city and is a common and prolific weed that has been used as a pot-herb, a medicine and a vegetable in the Middle East since ancient times.

2 CUPS YOUNG MALLOW LEAVES, WASHED AND FINELY CHOPPED

4 CUPS CHICKEN OR VEGETABLE STOCK

3 CLOVES GARLIC, CRUSHED

1 TABLESPOON OLIVE OIL

1 TEASPOON GROUND CORIANDER

PINCH CAYENNE PEPPER

1 TEASPOON TAMARI OR SOYA SAUCE

Place Mallow in stock, bring to boil, then reduce to simmer gently for 10 minutes. Meanwhile sauté garlic in oil until brown and then stir in coriander and cayenne. Mix into a paste with the tamari and add to the Mallow soup. Cover and simmer for about 3 minutes, stirring occasionally. Serve with crusty brown bread or a bowl of steamed brown rice. You can also turn this dish into a very nourishing meal by adding cooked meat or vegetables if you wish.

CARROT AND CHICKPEA SOUP – *Shurabat al Tahini* (Jordan)

1 CUP COOKED CHICKPEAS

2 CUPS CHOPPED CARROTS

2 CLOVES GARLIC, CRUSHED

1 SMALL ONION, FINELY CHOPPED

3 CUPS VEGETABLE STOCK

MINT, FRESH OR DRIED

1 TABLESPOON FRESHLY SQUEEZED LEMON JUICE

SEA SALT AND FRESHLY GROUND BLACK PEPPER, TO TASTE

3 TABLESPOONS YOGHURT

Place chickpeas in a pot with the carrots, garlic, onion and stock. Bring to the boil then reduce heat to simmer for about 20 minutes. Purée soup in a food processor or blender and then return to the pot. Add a little chopped mint, lemon juice, salt and pepper and simmer for a further 5 minutes. Serve garnished with yoghurt and mint.

HOT CARROT PICKLE – *Kabes el Havic (Jordan)*

500 g CARROTS

1 TABLESPOON BLACK MUSTARD SEEDS

1/2 TEASPOON FENNEL SEEDS

6 GREEN CHILLIS

3 CLOVES GARLIC, SLICED

1/2 TEASPOON SUGAR

SMALL PIECE GINGER ROOT, PEELED AND SLICED

1 TEASPOON SALT

250 ml WINE VINEGAR

Peel carrots then slice lengthways. Cut in half and place on a dish. Sprinkle with salt and leave for 24 hours in a warm place. Next day place carrots in a jar with the remaining ingredients, shake well and seal tightly. Store in a warm place for a week before using.

CHICKPEA SALAD – *Salata Nivik (Armenia)*

3 TABLESPOONS CHOPPED PARSLEY

3 TABLESPOONS FINELY CHOPPED ONION

2-3 CLOVES GARLIC, CRUSHED

½ LEMON, JUICED

3 TABLESPOONS OLIVE OIL

PINCH CAYENNE PEPPER

½ TEASPOON TAMARI

3 CUPS COOKED CHICKPEAS

Combine all ingredients, stirring well and serve at room temperature.

SHALLOT AND RADISH SALAD – *Salata Arabia (Saudi Arabia)*

3 SHALLOTS, FINELY CHOPPED

1 SMALL GREEN CAPSICUM, FINELY CHOPPED

1 SMALL BUNCH RADISHES, CHOPPED

SEA SALT, TO TASTE

PINCH CAYENNE PEPPER

PINCH PAPRIKA

2 TABLESPOONS LEMON JUICE

½ CUP YOGHURT

CHOPPED PARSLEY, TO GARNISH

Combine all ingredients, stirring well and serve at room temperature. Garnish with a little chopped parsley.

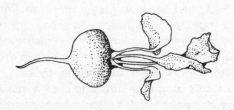

TOMATO AND CORIANDER SALAD –
Banadura Salata Bil Kizbara (Yemen)

3 TOMATOES, THINLY SLICED

1 SMALL CUCUMBER, THINLY SLICED

3 TABLESPOONS CORIANDER, FINELY CHOPPED

2 SHALLOTS, FINELY CHOPPED

2 SMALL HOT CHILLI, FINELY CHOPPED

SEA SALT AND FRESHLY GROUND BLACK PEPPER, TO TASTE

2 TABLESPOONS LEMON JUICE

3 TABLESPOONS OLIVE OIL

Combine vegetables with salt and pepper and pile into a salad bowl. Mix together lemon juice and olive oil and toss salad lightly before serving.

VEGETABLE KIBBI – Kibbi (Jordan)

1 CUP CRACKED WHEAT

2 CUPS HOT WATER

1½ CUPS CHICKPEAS, COOKED

PINCH NUTMEG

SALT AND PEPPER, TO TASTE

3 TABLESPOONS CHOPPED PARSLEY

PINCH CAYENNE PEPPER

3 TABLESPOONS OLIVE OIL

1 ONION, FINELY CHOPPED

1 TABLESPOON PINE-NUTS

Soak cracked wheat in 2 cups hot water for 10-15 minutes. Meanwhile, grate chickpeas. Squeeze excess moisture from cracked wheat and mix together with grated chickpeas. Stir in nutmeg, salt and pepper, parsley and cayenne pepper. Shape mixture into patties and place on a serving plate. Press a hole in the centre of each patty with fingers. Heat oil and gently sauté onions 5 minutes or until soft. Add pine nuts and cook a minute longer. Just before serving, spoon a little onion and pine nut mixture into the top of each patty.

STUFFED EGGPLANT – *Mahshi Batindshan Bi Zayt*
(Lebanon)

3 EGGPLANTS

1 CUP COOKED BROWN RICE

¼ CUP WALNUTS, CHOPPED

4 TABLESPOONS PARSLEY, CHOPPED

3 TABLESPOONS CHOPPED ONION

2 TOMATOES, PEELED AND CHOPPED

½ CUP OLIVE OIL

1 SMALL CAPSICUM, CHOPPED

SALT AND PEPPER, TO TASTE

2 TOMATOES, SLICED

Halve eggplants and scoop out with a sharp knife. Place brown rice, walnuts, parsley, onion, chopped tomatoes, oil, capsicum and seasoning in container and mix thoroughly. Fill eggplants with this mixture and top with tomato slices. Sprinkle with a little extra salt and pepper and place in a baking dish or heavy pan. Half cover with water and bake in a moderate oven or cook on top of the stove for 30 minutes. Uncover and allow the moisture to evaporate so that the sauce will thicken. Serve hot or at room temperature.

SESAME FISH – *Samak bi Tahini (Lebanon)*

1 kg FIRM WHITE FISH FILLETS

SALT

3 TABLESPOONS OLIVE OIL

2 ONIONS, CHOPPED

1½ CUPS TAHINI

⅜ TABLESPOONS LEMON JUICE

Sprinkle fish on both sides with salt and chill for 2 hours. Remove from fridge and place fish in an oiled baking dish, discarding the liquid that will have accumulated. Oil or butter a baking dish and place fish, brushed with olive oil under grill for 2-3 minutes per side. Sauté onions gently in remaining oil. When soft, stir in tahini and lemon juice, stirring well. Pour onion tahini sauce over fish and grill for a further 2-3 minutes or until the sauce bubbles and browns a little. Allow to cool to room temperature before serving. This dish can be baked rather than grilled, if preferred.

BRAISED BEANS – *Lubyi Bi Zayt (Lebanon)*

3 TABLESPOONS OLIVE OIL

1 ONION, FINELY SLICED

3 CLOVES GARLIC, CRUSHED

500 g TOMATOES, SKINNED AND CHOPPED

1 TABLESPOON TOMATO PASTE

SALT AND PEPPER, TO TASTE

½ TEASPOON HONEY

3 TABLESPOONS WATER

500 g GREEN BEANS, TOPPED, TAILED AND STRINGED

Heat oil and gently sauté onion and garlic 5 minutes. Stir in tomatoes, tomato paste, seasoning, honey and water and simmer gently for about 10 minutes. Add beans to the tomato mixture and simmer a further 20 minutes or until the beans are tender and most of the liquid is evaporated. Serve at room temperature.

PAPRIKA FISH CASSEROLE – *Yakhnit Samak Harrak*
(Lebanon)

1 kg WHITE FISH FILLETS

SALT

HEAD, BONES AND TAIL OF FISH

2 CUPS WATER

3 TABLESPOONS OLIVE OIL

1 ONION, FINELY CHOPPED

3 CLOVES GARLIC, CRUSHED

1 TEASPOON PAPRIKA

2 TEASPOONS FRESH CORIANDER, FINELY CHOPPED

A FEW CARAWAY SEEDS

3 TABLESPOONS LEMON JUICE

Sprinkle fish with salt and chill for at least two hours. Meanwhile, make stock by placing fish head, bones and tail in water. Bring to boil, then reduce to simmer for 20-30 minutes. Strain and set aside. When the fish is ready, heat oil in a large heavy pan and sauté fish on both sides till golden brown. Remove fish and reheat oil, then gently sauté onions and garlic. When they are soft, pour off the excess oil and add the fish stock to the onions. Add fish, paprika, coriander and caraway seeds and simmer for 15 minutes. Add the lemon juice, check seasoning — adding a little salt and pepper if liked — and then leave to cool. Serve at room temperature.

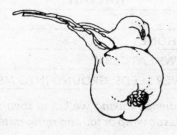

SAFFRON RICE – *Timman Z'affaran (Iraq)*

2 CUPS BASMATI RICE

4 CUPS WATER

½ TEASPOON SAFFRON THREADS

2 TABLESPOONS ROSE WATER

3 TABLESPOONS GHEE OR OIL

1 ONION, FINELY CHOPPED

½ TEASPOON GROUND CORIANDER

½ TEASPOON CUMIN SEEDS

½ TEASPOON NUTMEG

2 CARDAMOM PODS

3 TABLESPOONS ALMONDS, CHOPPED LENGTHWAYS

1 TABLESPOON PINE NUTS

1 TABLESPOON BLACK SULTANAS

Soak rice in water for half an hour. Pound saffron and place in a bowl with rose water. Heat ghee or oil and sauté onion with spices for 10 minutes over a low light, removing seeds from cardamom pods and discarding outer layers. Add almonds to spiced onion mixture and stir in 1 tablespoon rose water. Simmer gently for 15 minutes or so, adding the rest of the rose water just before serving. Serve garnished with pine nuts and sultanas.

HALVAH

¼ CUP TAHINI

3 TABLESPOONS HONEY

2 TABLESPOONS WHEATGERM

¼ CUP SUNFLOWER SEEDS, GROUND INTO MEAL

Combine all ingredients, mixing well, and then shape into two logs. Cover with plastic wrap or foil and refrigerate until required.

BAKED RICE PUDDING – *Shir Berenj (Iran)*

2 CUPS COOKED BROWN RICE

2 EGGS, LIGHTLY BEATEN

2 CUPS MILK

3 TABLESPOONS HONEY

½ TEASPOON CINNAMON

2 TABLESPOONS MAPLE SYRUP

½ TEASPOON NUTMEG

½ TEASPOON GROUND CARDAMOM

1 TABLESPOON ROSE WATER

1 TABLESPOON RAISINS (OPTIONAL)

Combine all ingredients and stir well. Pile into a buttered baking dish and bake for 30 minutes or until golden. Serve with yoghurt and a little extra honey or maple syrup.

MIDDLE EASTERN TAHINI CUSTARD

2 CUPS APPLE JUICE

2 TABLESPOONS HONEY

2 TABLESPOONS ARROWROOT

2 TABLESPOONS WATER

2 CARDAMOM PODS

6 TABLESPOONS TAHINI

1 TABLESPOON CHOPPED PISTACHIO NUTS

Place apple juice in a saucepan and bring to boil. Stir in honey and reduce to simmer gently. Make a paste with the arrowroot and water and stir into the apple juice. Add the seeds from the cardamom pods and the tahini and mix well. Pour the custard into a serving dish and garnish with pistachio nuts. Allow to cool to room temperature and then chill for at least 2 hours before serving.

SYRIAN DATE ROLLS – *Sambusik (Syria)*

½ TEASPOON CINNAMON
½ TEASPOON NUTMEG
2 CUPS WHOLEMEAL FLOUR
3 TABLESPOONS MELTED BUTTER
4 TABLESPOONS MILK
2 TABLESPOONS HONEY
3 TABLESPOONS GOOD QUALITY OIL
250g SEEDED DATES
3 TABLESPOONS BUTTER (EXTRA)
1 TEASPOON ROSE WATER

Add cinnamon and nutmeg to flour and then rub in butter until the mixture resembles breadcrumbs. Gently heat milk and stir in the honey. Leave to cool before adding to the flour. Stir in the oil at the same time and mix to form a soft dough. Knead the dough until smooth. To make the date filling, chop the dates finely and place in a saucepan with the extra butter. Leave over a very low light for 20-30 minutes, stirring from time to time so that the mixture does not catch, until it is soft and almost sloppy. Stir in the rose water and leave to cool a little. Roll the dough until it is about 5mm thick and then cut into small circles. Place a teaspoon of the date filling in the centre of each circle. Fold the circles in half to form crescents, pressing down with fingers or a fork. Place the date rolls on ungreased baking sheets and bake at 350°F (Gas 4) for 20-30 minutes or until lightly coloured. Cool on a wire rack and leave to cool before storing in an airtight container.

ARABIC YOGHURT CAKE (*Oman*)

1 CUP CORNMEAL

½ TEASPOON BAKING POWDER

¼ CUP ORANGE JUICE

¼ CUP HONEY

PINCH SALT

½ CUP YOGHURT

1 TABLESPOON BUTTER

1 TABLESPOON ROSE WATER

¼ TEASPOON CARDAMOM

Place cornmeal in a mixing bowl. Dissolve baking powder in orange juice and stir in honey, salt and yoghurt. Mix well and then stir into the cornmeal. Cover with a damp cloth and leave for 2 hours. After this time, pour the cake batter into a buttered lamington tin and bake for 30 minutes or until golden. Place butter, rose water and cardamom in a pan and heat gently to form a thin syrup. When the cake is cooked, cut it into eight sections, leaving it in the tin. Pour syrup evenly over the surface and leave to cool. Cut into smaller pieces to serve.

MIDDLE EASTERN YOGHURT DRINK – *Lassi*

½ CUP PLAIN YOGHURT

2½ CUPS ICED WATER

SALT AND PEPPER, TO TASTE

SPRIG MINT

ICE CUBES

Blend yoghurt and iced water with a whisk or in a blender until smooth. Season to taste with salt and pepper and pour into glasses over ice cubes. Garnish with mint and serve immediately. Alternatively, one can make a sweet lassi by substituting 2 teaspoons honey for the salt and pepper, and mineral water for the plain water.

JAPAN

Japanese cooking is unique. Delicate and subtle, refined and clean, it is always exquisitely presented. Appearance counts for a great deal in Japanese culture and food is no exception. Presentation is all important in this land where, reflecting the simple, understated art of the country, Japanese food is itself an art-form.

The sea is a great provider to the Japanese table, for more seafood is eaten there than in any other country in the world. All sorts of fish are eaten – from sea-urchins to sea-bass, as well as various types of seaweed and the irresistible but deadly fugu or blow-fish. The latter is served for one week each year in specially licensed restaurants, and each year a handful of people inevitably die from fugu poisoning. Despite the danger, fugu eating has survived for centuries in this country where a true delicacy is worth dying for.

The recipes which follow call for a variety of unusual ingredients that are now quite widely available in health food stores. These range from mirin, a sweet Japanese wine to sake, a drier rice wine; hearty soba or buckwheat noodles, and transparent shiitake noodles. All the dishes are simple to prepare, healthy to eat and beautiful to behold.

Authentic touches can be added with simple, colourful garnishes. Almost anything can be used. Pickled red ginger, jet black nori seaweed diced into thin black strips, soft green celery leaves, grated yellow egg yolks, sliced white horseradish and elaborately carved vegetables are all used to make Japanese cooking a very special art.

Experiment and adapt the cuisine to suit yourself. As long as it looks like a work of art, you'll know you're on the right track!

BASIC STOCK – *Dashi*

5 cm (2 INCH) PIECE *KOMBU* (DRIED KELP)

250 ml WATER

2 TEASPOONS *KATSUOBUSHI* DRIED BONITO (TUNA) FLAKES

Simmer the kelp and water together for a few minutes. Remove kelp and sprinkle in the dried bonito flakes. Bring to the boil and simmer for one minute then set aside for 2 minutes. Strain and discard bonito flakes. This stock can be kept in the fridge for 2-3 days.

TOFU AND MISO SOUP – *Tofu no Miso Shiru*

1 LITRE *DASHI* (BASIC STOCK)

4 TABLESPOONS DARK *MISO*

250 g TOFU, DICED

2 TABLESPOONS CHIVES, FINELY CHOPPED

Bring dashi to boil and reduce to simmer. Remove from heat and stir in miso. Put back on the stove, but do not allow to boil. Add the tofu and allow to heat through. Serve immediately, garnished with chives.

SUSHI RICE

3 CUPS SHORT-GRAIN RICE

4 CUPS WATER

5½ TABLESPOONS BROWN RICE VINEGAR

5 TABLESPOONS BROWN SUGAR

2 TABLESPOONS *TAMARI* OR SOYA SAUCE

Wash rice thoroughly then place in a heavy pan. Cover with water and bring to the boil. Reduce heat and simmer for 20 minutes or until all the liquid has evaporated. Let stand for a further 15 minutes. Meanwhile, place vinegar, sugar and tamari in a pot and heat slowly until the sugar dissolves. Place rice in a large dish, separating the grains with chopsticks. Sprinkle with cooled vinegar mixture so that the rice is sticky but not too mushy. This rice is used in many recipes.

SUSHI

4 CUPS SUSHI RICE

4 SLICES SMOKED SALMON

50 g WHITE FISH FILLETS

2 TEASPOONS MUSTARD

2 TABLESPOONS PICKLED RED GINGER, FINELY SLICED

PARSLEY, FINELY GRATED CUCUMBER SKIN, GRATED HORSE-
RADISH TO GARNISH

3 CUCUMBERS

125 g PRAWNS, SLICED

PINCH VEGISALT

2 TEASPOONS SOYA MAYONNAISE

Place waxed paper on the bottom of a Sushi pan or flat cake-tin.
Line the pan with cucumber slices, spread with a thin layer of
mustard. Pack a 5 cm (2 inch) layer of rice on top of the cucumbers
and push down with another pan. Leave for 10 minutes or more
then turn out onto a board. Remove the waxed paper and then
slice Sushi into squares. Repeat the process using prawns, mayonnaise and salted fish. Garnish with red ginger, parsley, grated
cucumber skin and horseradish.

SEAWEED RICE ROLLS – *Nori Maki*

Nori Rolls are a type of Sushi made by rolling Sushi rice in Nori
seaweed, with the aid of a small bamboo mat, known as a makisu.

To make Nori Rolls, take a sheet of Nori seaweed and wave it over
a flame for a few seconds. Place on a makisu or bamboo mat. If you
do not have one, substitute a clean tea towel. Place a tablespoon
or two of Sushi rice in the middle of the seaweed and spread
almost to the edges. Using your fingers, make a depression in the
centre of the rice. Fill this groove with strips of cucumber, raw
tuna, shiitake mushrooms or smoked salmon. Dress with a little
chopped umeboshi plum, grated horseradish or shredded ginger.
Roll up the filled seaweed, using the bamboo mat to help you.
Press the top and then remove from the mat. Slice each roll into
three pieces and eat as soon as possible.

TOFU OMELETTE – *Takara Yaki*

250g TOFU, DRAINED AND MASHED

5-6 MUSHROOMS, FINELY SLICED

250g CRABMEAT, FINELY CHOPPED

1 TEASPOON *MIRIN* OR COOKING SHERRY

½ TEASPOON *TAMARI* OR SOYA SAUCE

1 TABLESPOON PEAS (FROZEN OR FRESH)

1 TEASPOON WHOLEMEAL FLOUR, SIFTED

4 EGGS, LIGHTLY BEATEN

1 TEASPOON BUTTER

1 TEASPOON VEGETABLE OIL

Combine all ingredients except the butter and oil, mixing well. Heat butter and oil in a large pan. Pour in half the mixture and cover. Cook over a low heat for about 15 minutes or until all the egg has set. Set aside and keep warm and then repeat cooking process with the rest of the egg mixture. Slice cooked omelette into 25 × 50mm (1" × 2") bars. Serve hot with a little extra tamari and grated daikon (hot radish).

TOFU WITH GREEN MISO – *Tofu Dengaku*

250g TOFU, DRAINED AND CUT INTO 25 × 50mm (1" × 2") BARS

1 TABLESPOON *MISO*

2 TABLESPOONS *MIRIN* OR COOKING SHERRY

2 TABLESPOONS *DASHI* (BASIC STOCK – SEE ABOVE)

2 TABLESPOONS SPINACH PURÉE

Steam tofu pieces for 3-4 minutes. Meanwhile, place miso, mirin and dashi in a pot. Cook over low heat until a thin paste is formed then stir in the spinach purée. Spread tofu with the miso-spinach mixture. Place Tofu Dengaku *on bamboo skewers and serve hot as an appetiser.*

TEMPURA BATTER

This batter is used in a variety of dishes apart from Tempura.

½ BEATEN EGG

1 CUP COLD WATER

1 CUP FLOUR

Combine all ingredients and beat well. This is traditionally done with chopsticks although it can, of course, be mixed in a blender or food processor.

CHESTNUT RICE – *Kuri Gohan*

500g SHORT-GRAIN RICE

500g DRIED CHESTNUTS, SOAKED OVERNIGHT

1 LITRE WATER

1 TABLESPOON *MIRIN* OR SWEET SHERRY

1 TEASPOON TAMARI OR SOYA SAUCE

Wash the rice thoroughly and soak for one hour. Place chestnuts in a pan with the water and boil for 15 minutes. Add the rice, mirin and tamari and simmer for 20 minutes or until all the liquid is absorbed. Leave covered pot over a very low light for a further 15 minutes, then turn the heat off and leave 10 minutes longer. Serve hot.

RICE AND CLAMS – *Asari Gohan*

250g COOKED CLAMS, (FRESH OR CANNED) WITH THEIR LIQUID

4 CUPS SHORT GRAIN BROWN RICE

1 LEEK, FINELY CHOPPED

1 SHEET *NORI* TO GARNISH SEAWEED

Place the rice in a combination of clam juice and water. Bring to the boil and add chopped leeks and clams. Reduce to simmer and cook for 45 minutes or until all the moisture has been absorbed and the rice is tender. When cooked, leave pot covered for 5 minutes before serving. To garnish, wave nori over a flame for a few seconds to dry it. Cut into fine strips with scissors and sprinkle over rice. Serve hot.

SLICED RAW FISH – *Sashimi*

500g FRESH WHITE FISH FILLETS

1 TABLESPOON SEA SALT

2 TEASPOONS GREEN HORSERADISH (WASABE)

2 TEASPOONS WATER

3 TABLESPOONS *TAMARI* OR SOYA SAUCE

Sprinkle fish with salt, cover and refrigerate for 30 minutes. This makes the fish firmer and easier to slice. Using a very sharp knife, slice the fish crosswise and arrange on a serving plate. Combine horseradish and water to form a paste then stir in tamari. Serve Sashimi *with horseradish sauce.*

TEMPURA WITH BUCKWHEAT NOODLES – *Tempura Soba*

500g *SOBA* NOODLES

6 LARGE PRAWNS, SHELLED LEAVING THE TAIL INTACT

125g FIRM WHITE FISH, SLICED INTO 6 PIECES

1½ CUPS TEMPURA BATTER (SEE ABOVE)

VEGETABLE OIL FOR FRYING

6 CUPS *DASHI* (BASIC STOCK – SEE ABOVE)

125g MUNG BEANS SPROUTS

6 THIN SLICES LEMON TO GARNISH

Place soba *in a large pot. Cover with boiling water and simmer until* al dente, *ie cooked but not soft. Dust prawns and fish with flour then coat with the* Tempura *batter. Fry in hot oil for 4-5 minutes or until golden. Bring* dashi *to boil. Place bean sprouts in boiling stock, then remove from heat immediately. Place drained* soba *noodles in a serving dish. Cover with hot* dashi *and sprouts and arrange fried prawns and fish on top. Garnish with lemon twists and serve immediately.*

BARBECUED SARDINES – *Washi nosu Jyoyu Zuke*

4-5 TABLESPOONS *TAMARI* OR SOYA SAUCE

2 TABLESPOONS BROWN RICE VINEGAR

2 TABLESPOONS FRESHLY SQUEEZED LEMON JUICE

25mm (1") PIECE GINGER, CRUSHED IN A GARLIC CRUSHER

2 CLOVES GARLIC, CRUSHED

500g FRESH SARDINES, CLEANED AND GUTTED

2 TABLESPOONS VEGETABLE OIL

Place tamari, vinegar, lemon juice, ginger and garlic in a shallow dish, mixing well. Place sardines in the dish, basting with the marinade from time to time. Leave for 2-3 hours so that the sardines absorb all the flavours. Drain fish and wipe dry. Brush with half the oil and grill for 3-4 minutes. Turn, baste and grill the other side for 3-4 minutes then serve immediately.

FISH WITH BAMBOO SHOOT – *Nitsuke*

500g FIRM WHITE FISH FILLETS, DICED IN PIECES 25 × 50mm (1" × 2")

½ CUP *MIRIN* OR COOKING SHERRY

1 CUP *DASHI* OR BASIC STOCK

1 TABLESPOON BROWN SUGAR

2 TABLESPOONS *TAMARI* OR SOYA SAUCE

175g BAMBOO SHOOTS, FINELY SLICED

1 MEDIUM CARROTS, SLICED DIAGONALLY

125g STRINGLESS GREEN BEANS

Place fish in pan with mirin and dashi and simmer for 3-4 minutes. Sprinkle on sugar and tamari and cook for a further 5-7 minutes or until the fish is tender. Remove fish and set aside in a warm place. Cook bamboo shoots in the same pan for 2-3 minutes. Remove and set aside in a warm place. Simmer carrot for 2-3 minutes and remove. Finally, simmer beans for 2-3 minutes then cut in half. To serve, place fish and bamboo shoots in individual bowls, garnish with beans and carrots and serve hot.

JAPANESE FISH CAKES – *Kamoboko*

500g WHITE FISH FILLETS, MINCED

3 TABLESPOONS WHOLEMEAL FLOUR

2 EGG WHITES, BEATEN UNTIL WHITE AND FROTHY

1 TABLESPOON *MIRIN* OR COOKING SHERRY

1 TEASPOON HONEY

A LITTLE EXTRA FLOUR

3 TABLESPOONS VEGETABLE OIL

Mix together minced fish, flour, egg whites, mirin and honey. Shape mixture into small cakes, using about 2 tablespoons per cake. Dust fish cakes with extra flour and fry in the hot oil for 5 minutes per side or until the cakes are golden brown and crisp. Drain on absorbent paper and serve hot.

CHICKEN AND OYSTERS – *Yosenabe*

1 LITRE *DASHI* (BASIC STOCK)

2 CARROTS, SLICED DIAGONALLY

2 TABLESPOONS *TAMARI*

3 SHEETS *NORI* SEAWEED

12 PRAWNS, SHELLED

250g WHITE FISH FILLETS

8-10 DRIED JAPANESE BLACK MUSHROOMS, SOAKED IN COLD WATER FOR ½ HOUR

2 CHICKEN BREASTS, DICED

½ BUNCH RADISHES, SLICED

3 TABLESPOONS MIRIN

6 SHALLOTS, SLICED

18 RAW OYSTERS

100g *SHIRATAKI* NOODLES

Place dashi in a large pot and bring to the boil. Reduce heat and simmer chicken for 10 minutes. Add carrots and radishes and simmer for a further 5 minutes. Remove chicken and vegetables from pot and place on a serving dish. Bring stock back to boil and add tamari and mirin. Place diced nori, shallots, prawns, oysters, fish, noodles and mushrooms in boiling stock. Simmer for 4-5 minutes, then add chicken and vegetables. Heat through and serve at once.

CHICKEN TERIYAKI

4 TABLESPOONS *SAKE* OR COOKING SHERRY

2 TABLESPOONS *TAMARI* OR SOYA SAUCE

3 TABLESPOONS *MIRIN* OR SWEET WHITE WINE

6 TABLESPOONS *DASHI* OR BASIC STOCK

2 TEASPOONS BROWN SUGAR

4 CHICKEN BREASTS, SKINNED AND BONED

2 CELERY STALKS, SLICED LENGHTWISE

4 SHALLOTS, SLICED LENGTHWISE

Place sake in a small pot and warm gently. Remove from heat, then ignite. Allow the flames to die down naturally, then add tamari, mirin, dashi and sugar. Preheat griller to moderately hot. Dip chicken into marinade and grill for 5 minutes. Turn, basting the other side and continue to cook until golden brown. Turn again, baste liberally and cook initial side until golden. By basting generously, you should use up all the marinade. Serve chicken breasts sliced almost through. Pour on the hot juice, garnish with celery and shallots and serve hot.

PICKLED VEGETABLES – *Suzuke*

½ *DAIKON* JAPANESE RADISH

1½ CUPS BROWN RICE VINEGAR

⅛ TABLESPOON BROWN SUGAR

1 TEASPOON VEGISALT

TAMARI OR SOYA SAUCE

½ CHINESE CABBAGE

½ CUP *SAKE*

2 GARLIC CLOVES, CRUSHED

1 TEASPOON CRUSHED GINGER

Cut vegetables into bite-sized pieces and place in a wide mouthed jar or crock. Combine remaining ingredients and pour over vegetables. Cover with a plate and weigh down with a heavy object. Allow to stand for at least a day. To serve, sprinkle with tamari.

SESAME BEANS – *Goma Joyu-ae*

250g YOUNG GREEN BEANS, DIAGONALLY SLICED

4 TABLESPOONS SESAME SEEDS

1 TABLESPOON SESAME OIL

½ TEASPOON BROWN SUGAR

1 TEASPOON *MIRIN*

Steam beans until tender but still crunchy. Allow to cool while you make the dressing. Toast sesame seeds lightly then pound them in a mortar, adding the remaining ingredients gradually. Pour dressing over beans, toss well with chopsticks and serve.

CUCUMBER SALAD – *Kyurimoni*

4 SMALL CUCUMBERS

2 TABLESPOONS BROWN RICE VINEGAR

2 TEASPOONS SUGAR

1 TEASPOON DARK SESAME OIL

2 TEASPOONS SEA SALT

1 TEASPOON TAMARI

PINCH CAYENNE PEPPER

Peel cucumbers roughly, reserving some of the skin for garnish. Rub with salt then slice paper thin. This can be done in a food processor or with a vegetable peeler. Combine remaining ingredients and pour over cucumber slices. Toss well and leave for at least 30 minutes. Serve chilled.

BEAN SPROUT SALAD – *Kong Namool*

500 g MUNG BEAN SPROUTS

2 TEASPOONS *TAMARI* OR SOYA SAUCE

1 TABLESPOON SESAME SEEDS, TOASTED

1 TABLESPOON SESAME OIL

2 SHALLOTS, FINELY CHOPPED

1 TEASPOON BROWN RICE VINEGAR

½ TEASPOON HONEY

Place bean sprouts in a pot. Cover with boiling water and simmer for 3 minutes. Drain and set aside. Combine remaining ingredients and stir into bean sprouts, using chopsticks. This salad can be eaten hot or cold.

CARROT SALAD

4 CARROTS, SLICED INTO THICK JULIENNE STRIPS

2 *DAIKON* JAPANESE RADISHES, SLICED INTO THICK JULIENNE STRIPS

1 TEASPOON SEA SALT

4 TABLESPOONS BROWN RICE VINEGAR

1 TEASPOON HONEY

1 TABLESPOON *TAMARI* OR SOYA SAUCE

½ TEASPOON CRUSHED GINGER

1 TABLESPOON BLACK SESAME SEEDS

Place carrot and radish in a dish. Sprinkle with salt and leave for 1 hour. Drain vegetables and then dry on absorbent paper. Place remaining ingredients in a glass jar. Screw the lid on tightly and shake well. Pour dressing over the carrot and radish and serve at room temperature.

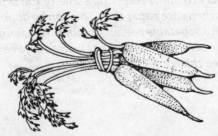

SPINACH SALAD – *Namoul*

1 BUNCH FRESH SPINACH

2 TABLESPOONS SESAME SEEDS, TOASTED

1 TABLESPOON SESAME OIL

1 TABLESPOON *TAMARI* OR SOYA SAUCE

2 SHALLOTS, FINELY CHOPPED

1 CLOVE GARLIC, CRUSHED (OPTIONAL)

PINCH CHILLI POWDER

Wash spinach thoroughly. Shake off excess water and place in a large pot. Cover and cook over a low light for 5-7 minutes or until tender. Combine remaining ingredients and set aside. Drain spinach and chop roughly. Stir dressing into spinach while it is still warm. This is best done with chopsticks. Serve at room temperature.

SWEET CHESTNUTS – *Kuri Kinto*

This dessert is traditionally served on New Year's Day in Japan.

250 WHITE SWEET POTATO, BOILED AND PURÉED

12 CANNED CHESTNUTS, HALVED

½ CUP SYRUP (FROM CANNED CHESTNUTS)

½ CUP WATER

1 TABLESPOON CORNFLOUR

Mould sweet potato into 12 little balls. Press two chestnut halves into each ball and set aside. Place chestnut syrup and water in a pan and bring to the boil. Simmer gently. Make a paste with the cornflour and some of the syrup. Return to pan and continue to simmer for 2-3 minutes. Pour syrup over chestnut balls and serve hot or cold.

FRIED CHESTNUTS – *Iga-Age*

These appetisers are quite beautiful to look at. Decorate with sprigs of pine for a most unusual effect.

FLOUR FOR DUSTING

½ CUP TEMPURA BATTER (SEE ABOVE)

12 WHOLE CHESTNUTS, COOKED AND PEELED (SWEET, CANNED ONES WILL DO)

125 g *SOMEN* OR ITALIAN STYLE *VERMICILLI*

LIGHT VEGETABLE OIL FOR FRYING

Dust chestnuts with flour and dip into tempura batter. Break somen *into 25mm (1") pieces. Roll battered chestnuts in* somen *and then deep fry in hot oil for a few minutes or until golden brown. Remove, drain on absorbent paper and serve immediately.*

WATERMELON BASKET – *Kori Suika*

1 SMALL, ROUND WATERMELON

1 PUNNET STRAWBERRIES, HULLED

1 LEMON, THINLY SLICED

ICE CUBES

Cut watermelon into the shape of a basket by removing the top third of the melon and just leaving rind for a 'handle'. Scoop out the melon and dice or shape into balls. Combine watermelon dice or balls, strawberries and ice cubes and return to watermelon basket. Garnish with lemon slices and serve chilled.

INDIA

The fragrant foods of India offer a variety of interesting and subtle tastes. Not just curry and rice, but breads (chapatis, parathas), *fritters* (samosas, pakorhas), *salads,* (raitas), *accompaniments* (sambals, pickles, chutneys) *and sweetmeats such as* halva.

The recipes which follow are not truly authentic for they contain whole foods wherever possible – a worthy concession to the new dietary wisdom of the Occident.

Fresh herbs and home-ground spices are usually superior to commercially dried herbs and pre-mixed curry powders, although there are some very good preparations available from health food shops and speciality stores.

The dishes which appear on the following pages can be served individually or in various combinations with plain brown or long grain Indian Basmati rice for a simple meal. Or, if you are feeling energetic and extravagant, prepare all the recipes for a festive Indian Banquet that will cater to all tastes.

THE MENU

Breads
Chapatis • Puris • Parathas

Appetisers
Samosas • Lentil Pakorhas

Main Courses
Chicken & Coconut Curry • Prawn Curry • Vegetable Curry
Spiced Cashews • Saag Dhal

Accompaniments
Cucumber Raita • Banana Raita • Sweet Pickles
Fresh Apple Chutney • Coriander Chutney

Vegetables
Alu Raita • Saag Alu

Grains
Rye Pilau • Golden Almond Rice

Desserts
Banana Halva • Sweet Potato Halva • Coconut Custard
Golden Fruit Salad • Saffron Yoghurt

CLARIFIED BUTTER – Ghee

Sold at many supermarkets and health food stores, ghee *is pure butter-fat without any of the milk solids. It can be heated to much higher temperatures than butter without burning, and imparts a distinctive flavour when used as a cooking medium. If you find it difficult to buy* ghee, *make your own by heating unsalted butter until it melts and froths. Spoon off foam from the top and pour the melted butter into a heatproof glass bowl, discarding the milk solids in the pan. Leave to cool to room temperature, then chill until set. Spoon off the fat from the top, leaving residue. Heat the fat again, then strain through fine muslin to remove any remaining solids.*

BREADS

UNLEAVENED WHOLEMEAL BREAD – *CHAPATIS*

This versatile bread can be used as an alternative to cutlery for scooping up curry and vegetables.

500 g WHOLEMEAL FLOUR

PINCH VEGISALT

1½ TABLESPOONS CORN OIL

200 ml WATER

Place flour and vegisalt into a bowl. Make a well in the centre and pour in oil and water. Mix to a soft dough, adding more water if necessary. Knead for ten minutes until the dough is smooth and elastic. Divide into balls, each the size of a walnut. Roll each one out on a well-floured board into thin circles, about the size and shape of a small French crepe. Do this until all the mixture has been used up. Meanwhile, heat a heavy frying pan thoroughly. Place a chapati in the pan and leave for a minute or so before turning. Press with a spatula or tea towel to encourage air to enter. Remove from pan and keep wrapped in a tea towel or cloth until all the chapatis are cooked and then serve warm.   Makes 24.

PURIS

These are similar to chapatis, but they are deep-fried and therefore both more delicious and less healthy!

AS FOR *CHAPATIS*

OIL FOR FRYING

Make as for chapatis. However, instead of dry-heating the pan, pour in enough oil to cover 25 mm (1") and heat. Put in the puris, one at a time, pressing with a spatula as they swell. Cook for one minute on each side or until golden. Drain on absorbent paper and serve warm.   Makes 15.

PARATHAS

Richer and more substantial than the chapati or puri, this bread is best served hot.

500 g WHOLEMEAL FLOUR
PINCH VEGISALT
200 ml WATER
250 g GHEE

Put the flour and vegisalt into a bowl and rub in 15g ghee with fingertips. Add water and knead as for chapatis. Set aside for one hour. Divide into ten pieces and shape each into balls. Flatten and roll into a circular shape until very thin. Melt remaining ghee and brush paratha lightly with the melted ghee. Fold the circle in half and brush again with ghee, then fold again. Roll the resultant triangle into a circle again and repeat the whole process three times. When all the parathas are ready, heat a frying pan with a knob of ghee. Place the parathas in the pan, one at a time, and cook on both sides until golden – about two minutes per side. Keep warm and serve immediately.   Makes 10.

PAPPADAMS

These fine lentil wafers are sold in many shops and make an excellent 'bread' accompaniment to any Indian meal. They cook in seconds and save a lot of time when you are cooking several other dishes.

APPETISERS
SPICED INDIAN PASTRIES – *Samosas*

These delicious little pastries are always very popular.
Chinese Spring-roll wrappers can be used instead of pastry for convenience.

Pastry:

250 g WHOLEMEAL FLOUR
1 TABLESPOON (25 g) GHEE
100 ml WARM WATER

Filling:

250g POTATOES

½ TEASPOON MUSTARD SEES

2 TABLESPOONS *GHEE* OR OIL

1 LARGE OR 2 SMALL ONIONS, FINELY CHOPPED

1 TEASPOON FRESH GINGER, GRATED

2 SMALL GREEN CHILLIES, FINELY CHOPPED

¼ TEASPOON TURMERIC

¼ TEASPOON CUMIN

1 TEASPOON GROUND CORIANDER *OR*
1½ TEASPOONS CURRY POWDER

PINCH VEGISALT

1 TABLESPOON LEMON JUICE

2 TEASPOONS FRESH CORIANDER, FINELY CHOPPED

Pastry

Rub ghee into flour, add water and make into a smooth dough. Knead for ten minutes then cover and set aside.

Filling

Scrub potatoes and dice. Boil until tender, then drain. Heat ghee or oil then add mustard seeds. When they start to pop, add onion, ginger and chillies and cook for 10 minutes over moderate heat until the onions are soft. Add turmeric, cumin and ground coriander and cook for a further 2 minutes, stirring all the time. Now add potatoes and vegisalt. Stir in lemon juice and coriander, then set aside to cool.

Samosas

Divide dough into ten pieces, shape into balls and roll out into thin circles. Cut each circle in half and place a good teaspoonful of the filling on one side of each half. Brush pastry edges with water then fold semi-circles in half and seal. Deep-fry the samosas in hot oil until golden and crisp. Drain and serve immediately. They are traditionally eaten with coconut or coriander chutney, (see below).

Makes 20.

LENTIL FRITTERS – *Lentil Pakorhas*

These little fritters can be served as part of the main meal or on their own in a sauce of whipped yoghurt, spiced with a pinch each of cayenne pepper and salt.

250 g RED LENTILS OR BESAN (LENTIL FLOUR)

1 TEASPOON FRESH GINGER, GRATED

2 CLOVES GARLIC, CRUSHED

½ TEASPOON CAYENNE PAPPER

½ TEASPOON TURMERIC

PINCH VEGISALT

2 TABLESPOONS FRESH CORIANDER

2 CUPS MIXED VEGETABLES, FINELY DICED CARROT, POTATO, EGGPLANT, (ZUCCHINI, OKRA OR CAPSICUM CAN BE USED)

If using lentils, wash and soak overnight. Next day, drain and then blend with ginger, garlic, cayenne, turmeric, vegisalt and coriander, gradually adding water until the mixture becomes smooth. Alternatively, if using besan, *add spices to the flour and then blend. Let the mixture stand 1 hour, then add the vegetables, mixing well. Heat oil and then drop large teaspoonsful of the mixture into pan. Cook a few at a time until golden – about one minute per side. Drain and serve immediately.*

MAIN COURSES

SPICED CASHEWS

Plump, soaked cashew nuts make this dish a delicacy.

250 g CASHEW NUTS

1 TABLESPOON *GHEE* OR OIL

2 LARGE ONIONS, FINELY SLICED

2 CLOVES GARLIC, CRUSHED

1 TABLESPOON HOT CURRY PASTE

5 CURRY LEAVES

3 PIECES LEMON GRASS, FRESH OR DRIED

500 ml COCONUT MILK

Soak raw cashews overnight in cold water. Next day, heat ghee or oil. Add onions, garlic and curry paste, stirring all the time for about 5 minutes over a low heat. Add curry leaves and lemon grass and then gradually pour in coconut milk. Simmer for 10 - 15 minutes to allow tastes to combine, then add drained cashews. Mix well and cook a further 5 minutes before serving.

SPINACH AND LENTIL PUREE – *Saag Dhal*

Dhal *is a basic food in India. Combined with spinach it makes a healthy, low fat dish bursting with protein and fibre. Use a fairly large pot as the spinach initially needs room.*

3 TABLESPOONS CORN OIL

2 ONIONS

3 GARLIC CLOVES

½ TEASPOON FRESH GINGER, GRATED

½ TEASPOON FENUGREEK SEEDS

½ TEASPOON CUMIN

½ TEASPOON GROUND CORIANDER

½ TEASPOON TURMERIC

PINCH SALT

PINCH CAYENNE PEPPER

500g RED LENTILS

2 TABLESPOONS ROUGHLY CHOPPED FRESH CORIANDER OR PARSLEY

1 TEASPOON *GARAM MASALA*

500g SPINACH OR SILVER BEET

Heat oil. Add onion and garlic. Stir well, then add ginger, fenugreek seeds, cumin, ground coriander, turmeric, salt and cayenne pepper. Cover and cook over low heat for 10 minutes. Add lentils and stir well. Barely cover with warm water and stir again. Cover pot and leave to cook slowly for about 10 - 15 minutes or until lentils are soft and mushy. Now stir in the fresh coriander and garam masala and allow to cook a further 2 minutes. Add the washed and roughly chopped spinach. Cover and allow spinach to cook in its own liquid for about 5 minutes, then stir into lentils.

VEGETABLE CURRY

You can use asparagus, beans, cauliflower, capsicums, potatoes, pumpkins, turnips or zucchinis for this recipe.

500 ml COCONUT MILK

2 ONIONS, ROUGHLY CHOPPED

1 GREEN CHILLI, FINELY CHOPPED

½ TEASPOON FRESH GINGER, GRATED

½ TEASPOON FRESHLY GRATED BLACK PEPPER

½ TEASPOON TURMERIC

2 CLOVES GARLIC, CRUSHED

2 CURRY LEAVES

1 TEASPOON *GARAM MASALA**

750 g MIXED VEGETABLES, ROUGHLY CHOPPED (SEE ABOVE)

2 TOMATOES, ROUGHLY CHOPPED

*This can be bought or made fresh (see following recipe)

Place coconut milk, onions, chilli, ginger, pepper, turmeric, garlic and curry leaves into pot and slowly bring to boil, stirring occasionally. Simmer gently for 10 minutes, adding more water only if the mixture starts to stick. Add remaining ingredients and cook a further 10 - 15 minutes or until vegetables are tender.

GARAM MASALA

Dry roast 1 tablespoon black peppercorns in a heavy-based pan. Remove and set aside. Repeat this process with ½ teaspoon whole cloves, 1 teaspoon cardamom seeds and 1 teaspoon fennel seeds respectively. Blend or pound in mortar and pestle with 1 cinnamon stick.

PRAWN CURRY

Made with fresh prawns, this dish is always a great favourite.

2 TABLESPOONS *GHEE* OR OIL

2 LARGE ONIONS, FINELY CHOPPED

8 CLOVES GARLIC, CRUSHED

2 TEASPOONS FRESH GINGER, GRATED

½ TEASPOON CUMIN SEEDS

1 TEASPOON POPPY SEEDS

1 PIECE LEMON GRASS, FRESH OR DRIED

1 CINNAMON STICK

1 TEASPOON CAYENNE PEPPER

1 TEASPOON SALT

125g CREAMED COCONUT

2 TABLESPOONS SHREDDED COCONUT

1 LEMON, JUICED

2 TABLESPOONS FRESH CORIANDER, FINELY CHOPPED

1kg LARGE PRAWNS, SHELLED AND DE-VEINED

Heat ghee or oil. Add onions, garlic, ginger, cumin and poppy seeds, lemon grass, cinnamon stick, cayenne and salt. Stir and cook over heat 10 minutes. Grate creamed coconut and add to mixture, stirring all the time. Add enough water or stock to make mixture liquid, but not too wet and then add shredded coconut, stirring constantly. Add prawns and leave to simmer for 20 minutes. Finally, add lemon juice and coriander. Stir well and serve with rice.

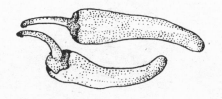

CHICKEN & COCONUT CURRY

The method used for this curry can be applied to many others, substituting meat, fish or vegetables such as eggplant or okra for the chicken.

1 CHICKEN, CUT INTO SMALL PIECES

OIL OR GHEE FOR FRYING

1 TABLESPOON BLACK MUSTARD SEEDS

1 TEASPOON CUMIN SEEDS

3 TABLESPOONS SHREDDED COCONUT

½ TEASPOON CAYENNE PEPPER

½ TEASPOON FRESH GINGER, GRATED

2 LARGE ONIONS, FINELY CHOPPED

2 GARLIC CLOVES, CRUSHED

Heat oil in large pot, then add chicken a few pieces at a time and fry until brown. Remove from heat and set aside. Into the same pot, place all the remaining ingredients and stir well, making sure everything is coated with a thin layer of oil. Cover pot and reduce heat to a low heat, allowing the onions and spices to stew for 15 - 20 minutes. Check occasionally to prevent sticking. When the onions are golden, add the chicken and stir well. Add enough warm water or stock to cover the chicken, turn up the heat and stir again. Reduce heat when water has boiled, cover pot and leave to simmer for one hour, adding more water only if necessary. The curry is ready when the water becomes a thick sauce and the meat falls easily from the bones.

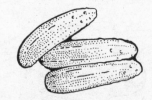

ACCOMPANIMENTS

CORIANDER CHUTNEY

If fresh coriander is unavailable, substitute mint for this aromatic chutney.

SMALL BUNCH FRESH CORIANDER, FINELY CHOPPED
7 SPRING ONIONS OR SHALLOTS, FINELY CHOPPED
2 FRESH GREEN CHILLIES, SEEDED AND FINELY CHOPPED
1/2 TEASPOON VEGISALT
1 TEASPOON BROWN SUGAR
1 TEASPOON *GARAM MASALA*
1 LEMON, JUICED
2-3 TABLESPOONS WATER

Blend all ingredients gradually in a mortar and pestle or in an electric blender if you have one. Put into a dish and chill.

CUCUMBER RAITA

This well-known cucumber salad is cool and refreshing – a welcome, almost essential part of any Indian meal.

2 LARGE CUCUMBERS
250 ml NATURAL YOGHURT
1/2 TEASPOON SALT
1/2 TEASPOON GROUND CUMIN
1/2 TEASPOON CUMIN SEEDS
1 TEASPOON CIDER VINEGAR
2 TABLESPOONS FRESH MINT OR CORIANDER, FINELY CHOPPED

Peel cucumbers, sprinkle with salt and set aside 30 minutes. Meanwhile mix together all remaining ingredients, reserving a fresh sprig of mint or coriander. When cucumbers have sweated 30 minutes, drain, then chop roughly. Add to yoghurt mixture, stirring well. Leave for an hour so that the flavours have time to blend. Garnish with mint or coriander sprig.

BANANA RAITA

Sweet and light—this simple accompaniment to the main meal is also delicious served with yoghurt as a dessert.

4 BANANAS

1 LEMON, JUICED

2 TABLESPOONS SHREDDED COCONUT

Peel and slice the bananas. Toss in lemon and coconut, transfer to a pretty dish and garnish with wedges of lemon.

SWEET PICKLES

There are many good pickles and chutneys available in the shops. However, if you wish to make your own, this recipe is ideal. Prepare the pickles at least two days before you need to use them to give the spices time to blend and settle.

3 TABLESPOONS CORN OIL

3 CLOVES GARLIC, CRUSHED

1 TEASPOON GRATED FRESH GINGER

2 ONIONS, SLICED

½ TEASPOON CAYENNE PEPPER

½ TEASPOON CUMIN SEEDS

½ TEASPOON TURMERIC

½ TEASPOON GROUND CLOVES

½ TEASPOON VEGISALT

500g YOUNG TURNIPS, FINELY SLICED

250g CARROTS, FINELY SLICED

250g CAULIFLOWER, BROKEN INTO FLORETS

125g BROWN SUGAR

250ml WINE VINEGAR

Heat oil. Add garlic, ginger and onion and cook 5 minutes. Add spices and cook a further 5 minutes, stirring well. Allow to cool then add sliced turnips and carrots and cauliflower pieces. Mix sugar and vinegar and bring to boil. Remove from heat and, when cool, pour over vegetables. Cover and leave for at least 2 days.

FRESH APPLE CHUTNEY

Use tart green apples for this fresh chutney. Green mangoes can also be treated in the same way.

3 GREEN APPLES

1 LEMON, JUICED

1 TEASPOON SALT

1 TEASPOON CHILLI POWDER

1 TEASPOON FRESH CORIANDER, FINELY CHOPPED

Peel and slice the apples. Combine with remaining ingredients and serve immediately. NOTE: The apples tend to go brown if left standing too long.

VEGETABLES

Saag Alu

A nutritious, tasty blend of spinach and potato, this vegetable dish combines well with curry and grains.

2 TABLESPOONS OIL OR *GHEE*

2 ONIONS, CHOPPED

3 CLOVES GARLIC, CRUSHED

1/2 TEASPOON FRESH GINGER, GRATED

1 TEASPOON BLACK MUSTARD SEEDS

1 TEASPOON CUMIN SEEDS

1 TABLESPOON CURRY PASTE – HOT OR MILD, AS YOU PREFER

PINCH VEGISALT

1 kg POTATOES, COOKED AND DICED

500 g SPINACH OR SILVER BEET, ROUGHLY CHOPPED

Heat oil or ghee. Add onions, garlic and ginger and cook over low heat 5 - 10 minutes before adding spices. Mix thoroughly, add potatoes and keep stirring. Add the spinach and stir again. Cover pot and cook for a further 5 minutes until spinach is done.

POTATO SALAD – *Alu Raita*

This spicy potato salad has a definite Indian flavour. Its bland ingredients make it a perfect foil for hotter dishes.

500 g POTATOES, COOKED AND SLICED
250 g TOMATOES, SLICED
FRESHLY GROUND BLACK PEPPER
PINCH VEGISALT
½ TEASPOON CUMIN SEEDS
½ TEASPOON CIDER VINEGAR
500 ml NATURAL YOGHURT
2 TABLESPOONS FRESH CORIANDER, CHOPPED

Mix potatoes and tomatoes. Then combine pepper, vegisalt, cumin seeds, vinegar and yoghurt, mixing well. Fold through potatoes and tomatoes. Transfer to serving dish and garnish with fresh coriander.

GRAINS
RYE PILAU

An interesting change from rice.

100 g CRACKED RYE
250 g BROWN LENTILS, SOAKED OVERNIGHT
2 ONIONS
2 TABLESPOONS *GHEE* OR OIL
1 TEASPOON CARAWAY SEEDS
½ TEASPOON SAFFRON THREADS
5 PEPPERCORNS
2 WHOLE CLOVES
3 CARDAMOM PODS, BRUISED
1 CINNAMON STICK
3 TABLESPOONS TOASTED ALMONDS, ROUGHLY CHOPPED

Wash rye then dry toast for a few minutes. Add 1 litre of water, simmer 45 minutes and then drain. Meanwhile, simmer lentils separately in 1 litre of water until cooked, about 30 minutes, and then drain. Slice onions and fry in oil for a couple of minutes before adding spices and seasonings. Add rye and lentils. Moisten with water if the mixture is very dry. Mix well, then transfer to a lightly oiled casserole dish. Cover and bake in a moderate oven (350°F, 180°C) for 25 minutes. Garnish with a little raw onion if desired.

GOLDEN ALMOND RICE

400 g BASMATI RICE

2 TABLESPOONS *GHEE*

2 ONIONS, FINELY SLICED

4 WHOLE CLOVES

6 CARDAMOM PODS, BRUISED

1 STICK CINNAMON

½ TEASPOON TURMERIC

½ TEASPOON VEGISALT

750 ml CHICKEN OR VEGETABLE STOCK

2 TABLESPOONS ALMONDS, TOASTED AND CHOPPED

2 TABLESPOONS COOKED PEAS

Wash rice thoroughly and drain. Heat ghee. Add onion and cook until golden then add drained rice and remaining spices. Stir well and cook over low heat for 5 - 10 minutes. Add stock. Bring to the boil then cover and reduce to simmer for 20 minutes. When cooked, leave uncovered for 5 minutes before removing cinnamon stick and cardamom pods. Garnish with peas and almonds.

DESSERTS

BANANA HALVA

This dessert can be served either hot or cold.

5 TABLESPOONS BUTTER OR *GHEE*

10 LARGE, FIRM BANANAS

1 CUP WATER

3 TABLESPOONS HONEY

1 TEASPOON GROUND CARDAMOM

2 TABLESPOONS ALMONDS, BLANCHED AND CHOPPED

½ TEASPOON ROSE WATER

PINCH NUTMEG

Melt butter and poach sliced bananas slowly, then mash with potato masher. Add water and honey and cook over low heat, stirring continuously until the mixture becomes thick and creamy. Remove from heat, add cardamom, almonds and rose water, and beat well. Pour into glass dish and sprinkle with nutmeg.

COCONUT CUSTARD

2 LARGE EGGS (FREE RANGE ARE BEST)

50g BLACK SUGAR

50ml MAPLE SYRUP

200ml COCONUT CREAM (AVAILABLE IN CANS)

PINCH GROUND CARDAMOM

PINCH GROUND CLOVES

PINCH NUTMEG

2 TEASPOONS ROSE WATER

Beat eggs lightly, then add sugar, maple syrup, coconut cream and enough water to make the mixture a little runny, but still thick – about 3 - 4 tablespoons. Add spices and rose water and mix well. Pour into buttered casserole dish and place in baking dish filled with water. Bake in a slow oven 300°F for 2 hours. Custard is done when a skewer comes out clean. Leave to cool and serve chilled with a little whipped cream.

SAFFRON YOGHURT

This dish can be served either with or after the meal.

500 g NATURAL YOGHURT

2 TABLESPOONS MAPLE SYRUP

½ TEASPOON SAFFRON THREADS

3 TABLESPOONS CHOPPED PISTACHIO NUTS

Line a colander with muslin and place over a bowl. Pour in the yoghurt and leave for a few hours until no more whey drips out. Turn the curds into a bowl. Put the saffron threads in a cup and add a tablespoon of hot water to dissolve them. Add this and the maple syrup and 1 tablespoon of pistachio nuts to the yoghurt curds. Beat well. Serve in small bowls and garnish with remaining nuts.

NOTE: Don't throw out the whey. It can be used in place of stock in many of the above dishes, especially the Chicken & Coconut Curry, Prawn Curry and Saag Dhal.

GOLDEN FRUIT SALAD

This is not an Indian dish at all really, but it makes an excellent dessert after a rich, spicy meal.

1 MEDIUM-SIZED PAPAYA, PEELED AND CHOPPED

1 RIPE ROCK MELON, PEELED AND DICED

3 ORANGES, JUICED

3 RIPE PEACHES, PEELED AND SLICED

2 BANANAS, PEELED AND SLICED

½ CUP DATES, PITTED AND CHOPPED

½ CUP PECAN NUTS OR WALNUTS

1 KIWI FRUIT, PEELED AND SLICED

Combine all ingredients except kiwi fruit and place into a glass bowl. Chill. Before serving, garnish with slices of kiwi fruit.

SWEET POTATO HALVA

*Sweet potato halva is rich, sweet and sticky. Serve small,
diamond-shaped pieces with tea or coffee at the end of the meal.*

250 g BROWN SUGAR

250 ml MILK

1 × 400 g CAN SWEETENED CONDENSED MILK

4 TABLESPOONS BUTTER OR *GHEE*

250 g SWEET POTATO, COOKED AND MASHED

250 g CHOPPED PISTACHIO NUTS

2 TABLESPOONS ROSE WATER

1 TEASPOON GROUND CARDAMOM

*Place sugar, milks and butter in a large, heavy saucepan and cook
over low heat, stirring continuously until the mixture reaches
'soft ball stage', (ie place a tiny amount of the mixture in a saucer
full of cold water. If it forms a soft ball, then it is ready.) Remove
from heat and add sweet potato and pistachio nuts. Return to
heat and bring back to soft ball stage again. Remove from heat
and add remaining ingredients. Mix well and then pour into a
greased shallow dish. Press down with a fork and leave to set.*

SOUTH-EAST ASIA

China ● Vietnam ● Indonesia

The key to successful Asian cookery lies in its subtlety. Carefully prepared and speedily cooked, the flavours remain intact – clear and distinct.

Woks (Asian frypans) are designed to give maximum heat so that vegetables can be cooked quickly and thus retain their nutrients. Many Asian foods are lightly steamed in bamboo baskets, whilst others are eaten raw.

Meat is eaten in small amounts – tofu (bean curd) and seaweed provide a healthy basis for many recipes, as both these ingredients contain a good range of nutrients.

Food is scarce in Asia, so nothing is ever wasted – a cauliflower provides white florets for one meal and green stems which can be sliced and lightly cooked for another; a chicken provides meat from its flesh, soup and stock from its bones.

The food is gently flavoured with aromatic herbs like coriander and Vietnamese mint; seasoned with miso and tamari; spiced with garlic and chilli. These ingredients are all available – at Chinatown or in health food stores.

Authentic Asian food is not always nutritious, but if we exchange brown rice for white, tamari for soya sauce and leave out the M.S.G., we can have healthy, appetising meals.

M.S.G.

Monosodium glutamate is a chemical flavour intensifier commonly used in commercial oriental cooking. It causes an allergic reaction in some people, the symptoms ranging from flushing, burning sensations and in some cases serious illness. There is some evidence that a deficiency in Vitamin B_6 exaggerates one's reaction to M.S.G. However, freshly cooked Asian foods with low salt tamari are preferable as M.S.G. is another source of sodium, of which we all tend to have too much and which contributes to high blood pressure.

Here is a medley of classic Asian dishes, only slightly adapted to make them good for you. Most of the recipes are full of vitamins and minerals, even though animal products are so little used. They are colourful and inexpensive – you don't need elaborate ingredients or equipment to make these almost-authentic Asian dishes.

Their success lies in their simplicity, and their appeal reflects the serenity of the cook. So, experiment and enjoy!

EGG FLOWER SOUP (China)

This dish has a lot going for it. Not only is it a light, easy-to-prepare, good-looking soup, it is also highly nutritious.

1 LITRE CHICKEN STOCK
1 TABLESPOON TAMARI
PINCH CHILLI POWDER OR CAYENNE
2 TABLESPOONS CHOPPED SHALLOTS
2 LIGHTLY BEATEN EGGS

Bring stock to boil. Add tamari and chilli powder or cayenne. Simmer 5 minutes then very slowly pour eggs into soup. Serve immediately, garnished with chopped shallots.

VIETNAMESE MINT SOUP (Vietnam)

This soup is flavoured with Vietnamese mint (if you can find it). Coriander can be used as a substitute as it also imparts a delicate aroma to this delicious soup.

500 ml CHICKEN STOCK
250 g CHOPPED TOFU
125 g DICED, COOKED CHICKEN
1 TABLESPOON CHOPPED VIETNAMESE MINT OR CORIANDER
2 TABLESPOONS TAMARI
PINCH CAYENNE

Bring stock to boil. Add tofu and chicken. Season with tamari and cayenne and garnish with mint. Serve at once.

CRAB OMELETTE (Vietnam)

It's the coriander that gives this dish its Asian flavour. Serve with slowly cooked brown rice and perhaps a glass of crisp white wine (or apple juice if you prefer).

4 EGGS
TAMARI TO TASTE
CHILLI POWDER
½ COOKED CRAB, FLAKED
3-4 CHOPPED SHALLOTS
5-6 COOKED MUSHROOMS, SLICED
2 TABLESPOONS CORN OIL
CORIANDER FOR GARNISH
LEMON WEDGES

Beat eggs and season with tamari and chilli powder to taste. Heat 1 tablespoon oil and sauté shallots till golden. Add crab and heat through. Remove this mixture and put aside. Heat remaining oil, then add eggs, drawing in from sides of pan as it cooks. Place crab and shallot mixture on the almost-cooked omelette and then fold over. Turn out onto a warmed dish, garnish with lemon and coriander and serve immediately. An omelette waits for no-one wherever it comes from!

MARINE LIME SALAD (S.E. Asia)

500 g WHITE FISH FILLETS, FINELY CHOPPED

½ CUP LIME JUICE (OR LEMON)

3-4 SHALLOTS, THINLY SLICED

2 CLOVES CRUSHED GARLIC

1 TABLESPOON TAMARI

1 FRESH, THINLY SLICED HOT CHILLI

CORIANDER FOR GARNISH (OR MINT)

A FEW LETTUCE LEAVES

Place chopped fish in dish and cover with lime juice. Refrigerate overnight. Next day, add shallots, garlic, tamari and chilli. Serve on a bed of lettuce leaves. Garnish with coriander or mint.

SWEET & SOUR CRAB (China)

2 LARGE FRESH CRABS

1 ONION

1-2 CLOVES CRUSHED GARLIC

1 FINELY CHOPPED HOT CHILLI

1 TEASPOON FINELY CHOPPED FRESH GINGER

4 TABLESPOONS VEGETABLE OIL

½ CUP STOCK

2 TABLESPOONS WHITE VINEGAR

1 TABLESPOON HONEY

1 TABLESPOON TAMARI

1 TABLESPOON WHOLEMEAL FLOUR

Clean crab and cut into pieces. Chop onion and fry with garlic, chilli and ginger for 2 minutes. Then fry crab pieces till they change colour. Pour in stock, cover and simmer ¼ hour. Add vinegar, honey and tamari. Make flour into paste with some of the liquid in the pan and then add this mixture to the dish. Cook a further 5 minutes.
This crab can be served hot or cold.

DRAGON VEGIES (China)

These Chinese vegetables are crisp and their colours are bright and clear because they are only briefly cooked. The delicate flavouring gives them their Chinese hallmark and the variety gives them their name – for in Chinese mythology, the dragon is the luckiest sign in the zodiac. Eat these vegies with lucky rice and you won't be able to avoid good fortune!

½ CUP BROCCOLI FLORETS AND THINLY SLICED STEMS

½ CUP CAULIFLOWER FLORETS AND THINLY SLICED STEMS

½ CUP SNOW PEAS

1 TABLESPOON OIL – SESAME OR CORN

1 CLOVE CRUSHED GARLIC

1 TABLESPOON CRUSHED, FRESH GINGER

1 CUP SLICED MUSHROOMS

1 SMALL CAN WATER CHESTNUTS

½ CUP RAW CASHEW NUTS

4 TABLESPOONS VEGETABLE OR CHICKEN STOCK

1 TABLESPOON TAMARI

CHILLI OR CAYENNE TO TASTE

Blanch cauliflower, broccoli and peas quickly in boiling water, then plunge into iced water so that they retain their colour. Heat oil in wok, add garlic and ginger. Sauté mushrooms, water chestnuts, cashew nuts and blanched vegetables for a minute. Add stock, tamari and chilli and simmer for a couple of minutes with the lid on.

INDONESIAN BEAN DELIGHT (Indonesia)

This crunchy mixture of beans and bean sprouts is a highly spiced dish and makes a perfect accompaniment for blander rice dishes.

500g FRESH BEAN SPROUTS (MUNG)

500g FRESH GREEN BEANS – DIAGONALLY SLICED

1 TABLESPOON FRESH GINGER – GRATED

2 CLOVES CRUSHED GARLIC

1 TABLESPOON TAMARI

PINCH CAYENNE

2 FINELY SLICED ONIONS

1 TABLESPOON OIL

2 TABLESPOONS VEGETABLE STOCK

Heat oil in wok and sauté onions. Add garlic, ginger and cayenne, beans and stock. Cover and cook a few minutes. Add bean sprouts and tamari and heat through. This dish can be served either hot or cold.

ORIENTAL SURPRISE (China)

This gently simmered dish has a distinctive Chinese flavour. Try to get fresh ingredients if they are available – otherwise use tins or packets to make this tasty meal.

12-13 CHINESE MUSHROOMS

2 TABLESPOONS CHINESE WOOD FUNGUS

250g BAMBOO SHOOTS

500g BABY CORN COBS

250g SLICED WATER CHESTNUTS

3 TABLESPOONS SESAME OIL

2 TABLESPOONS TAMARI

1 TEASPOON GRATED FRESH GINGER

1 TABLESPOON HONEY

Soaks mushrooms in hot water 1 hour. Remove and dry, reserving liquid. Soak wood fungus 1/4 hour, then rinse, drain and chop. Thinly slice bamboo shoots. Drain corn. When all ingredients are

*thus prepared, heat the oil in a wok. Fry the mushrooms for about
5 minutes, stirring constantly. Add all other ingredients except
the wood fungus and simmer with 2 cups of reserved mushroom
liquid for ½ hour.*
Add wood fungus and serve with sesame rice.

ORIENTAL SPICED CHICKEN (China)

1.5 kg CHICKEN PIECES

½ CUP TAMARI

¼ CUP SESAME OIL

1 TABLESPOON DRY SHERRY

2 CLOVES CRUSHED GARLIC

½ TEASPOON FINELY GRATED GINGER

¼ TEASPOON SEA SALT

2 TEASPOONS FIVE SPICE POWDER

1 TABLESPOON HONEY

Wash and dry chicken pieces.

*Mix tamari, oil, sherry, garlic, ginger, salt and five spice powder.
Add chicken to marinade and steep at least 1 hour. Remove chicken, put in dish and spoon over 2 tablespoons of liquid. Bake in
moderate oven 1 hour until chicken is golden and crispy, basting
every 20 minutes. Serve hot or cold.*

GADO GADO (Indonesia)

This classic Indonesian salad is colourful and tasty. Arrange the vegetables carefully for maximum appeal.

3 POTATOES, THICKLY SLICED

3 CARROTS, SLICED DIAGONALLY

500g GREEN BEANS, SLICED DIAGONALLY

250g FRESH MUNG BEAN SPROUTS

SMALL BUNCH WATERCRESS

2 SMALL CUCUMBERS, SCORED WITH A FORK AND THINLY SLICED

3 HARD BOILED EGGS

1 CUP FINELY SHREDDED LETTUCE

1 CUP FINELY SHREDDED CABBAGE

Steam potatoes, carrots and beans until tender, but still firm. Set aside and allow to cool. Blanch cabbage in boiling water 1-2 minutes, drain and cool with cold water.

Put washed watercress on a large plate and arrange remaining vegetables individually on top. Surround with cucumber slices and serve with peanut sauce.

PEANUT SAUCE (Indonesia)

2 CUPS PEANUTS, BLENDED

1 CUP PEANUT BUTTER

2 CLOVES CRUSHED GARLIC

1 TEASPOON DRIED SHRIMP PASTE (TRASI), OPTIONAL

1 TABLESPOON LEMON JUICE

1 TABLESPOON TAMARI

1 TABLESPOON CHILLI, FINELY CHOPPED OR PINCH CHILLI POWDER

1/2-1 CUP COCONUT MILK

1 TABLESPOON PEANUT OIL

1 TABLESPOON HONEY

Heat oil and sauté garlic, trasi and chilli. Stir in peanuts or peanut butter and coconut milk over gentle heat until a thick pouring consistency is reached. Remove from heat and add lemon juice, honey and tamari.

LUCKY RICE (China)

3 CUPS COOKED BROWN RICE

2 TABLESPOONS VEGETABLE OIL

3 EGGS, LIGHTLY BEATEN

2 TABLESPOONS TAMARI

500g COOKED CHICKEN OR COOKED VEGETABLES

1 RED CAPSICUM, FINELY CHOPPED

A FEW TOASTED ALMONDS

FEW SPRIGS CORIANDER

Heat oil and add beaten eggs. When nearly set, add rice and fry for 5 minutes, stirring all the time. Add chopped chicken or vegies, capsicum and tamari and fry another 5 minutes. Serve sprinkled with toasted almonds, garnished with coriander.

SESAME RICE

3 CUPS BROWN RICE

6 CUPS WATER

1 CUP SESAME SEEDS

3 SHALLOTS

OIL FOR FRYING

PARSLEY FOR GARNISH

1 TABLESPOON TAMARI

Bring rice to boil in water, then reduce heat and simmer 40-45 minutes or until all water is absorbed. Meanwhile put sesame seeds in heavy pan over medium heat. Stir continuously until sesame seeds are golden. Remove from pan. Heat oil in pan and then add chopped shallots. When cooked add rice and sesame seeds. Season with tamari and sprinkle with chopped parsley.

SOY RICE

2 CUPS BROWN RICE

2 CUPS SOYA GRITS

6 CUPS WATER

Put rice and soya grits into cold water. Bring to boil, then reduce heat and simmer 45 minutes, or until all water absorbed.

CHINESE TEA

The perfect way to end an Asian meal is with a subtle, amber-coloured cup of Chinese tea. There are several kinds of tea, but only one species. That is to say, tea leaves are subjected to various processes which result in different classification of types, such as black, green or oolong. These can then be flavoured with petals of jasmine, chrysanthemum, lychee or rose to provide the fragrant beverage that helps soothe the system and aids digestion.

To make a perfect cup of Chinese tea, don't forget to warm the pot. Allow 1 tablespoon tea leaves for each litre of boiling water. Let the infusion stand for about 5 minutes and drink the tea as it is – without milk or sugar – so that its delicate flavour can be appreciated.

U.S.A.

From the mooseburgers and barbecued reindeer of Alaska to the famed Shoe-fly and Apple Pan Dandy of the Deep South, American cooking is both varied and unique. The recipes which appear below are representative of the cuisine of the United States, although much has not been included. Hawaiian pit-roasted kukui nuts, 'Tex-Mex' dishes from the hot south-western states, fried Oklahoma squirrel and Maryland terrapins are all popular regional dishes, but they somehow seem more appropriate in their own home towns. However, ingredients such as fresh fruit and vegetables which feature in Californian cooking and the sea food of New England have international appeal. Hence, the emphasis here is on the modern flavour of fresh, light North American fare rather than on the wild turkey and tough hogs and boars eaten by the pioneers!

CORN BREAD

A great American standby, usually served hot with butter and tasty cheese.

500g YELLOW CORN MEAL

250g WHOLEMEAL FLOUR

1 TABLESPOON BAKING POWDER

PINCH VEGISALT

250ml MILK

2 EGGS

3 TABLESPOONS COLD PRESSED OIL

3 TABLESPOONS HONEY

Mix together corn meal, flour, baking powder and salt. In another bowl, mix together milk, eggs, oil and honey. Pour wet mixture into dry ingredients and stir well. Pour batter into a greased baking tin and bake at 350°F/180°C for 30-35 minutes or until golden brown and firm.

NOTE This recipe calls for the use of a shallow baking tin. However, if you prefer to make a loaf, use a bread tin and cook for an extra 15 minutes.

DEEP SOUTH CORN SOUP

2 TABLESPOONS BUTTER

2 TABLESPOONS FLOUR

500ml MILK

500ml CHICKEN OR VEGETABLE STOCK

2 CUPS CORN KERNELS (FRESH OR TINNED)

1 TEASPOON TAMARI OR SOYA SAUCE

¼ TEASPOON CHILLI POWDER

FRESH POPCORN, TO GARNISH

Melt butter and stir in the flour. Cook for a couple of minutes then gradually add milk and stock and stir constantly until soup thickens. Add corn, tamari and chilli powder and simmer gently for 10-15 minutes. Garnish with unsweetened popcorn or croutons.

CUCUMBER BISQUE WASHINGTON

2 TABLESPOONS BUTTER

1 LARGE ONION FINELY CHOPPED

2 CUCUMBERS, PEELED AND CHOPPED

500 ml CHICKEN OR VEGETABLE STOCK

2 POTATOES, DICED

1 TABLESPOON BUTER

1 TABLESPOON FLOUR

2 EGG YOLKS

125 ml CREAM OR YOGHURT

1 EXTRA CUCUMBER

1 TEASPOON VEGISALT

PINCH WHITE PEPPER

CHIVES, TO GARNISH

Melt butter and gently sauté onion tili soft. Add cucumbers, cook for a couple of minutes, and then add stock and potatoes and simmer until tender. This takes about 15-20 minutes. Pureé soup by pushing through a sieve. Melt extra butter and stir in flour. Cook for a couple of minutes and then gradually add the warm purée, beating all the time. Simmer 5 minutes until the soup thickens a little. Beat egg yolks and cream or yoghurt. Add a little of the hot soup to the egg yolk mixture and then add it to the soup. Simmer 5 minutes but do not allow to boil. Add the extra cucumber, finely chopped, and also the vegisalt and pepper. Garnish with chives and serve hot or cold.

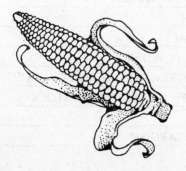

NEW ENGLAND CLAM CHOWDER

This soup is traditionally cooked with salted belly of pork, although it is pefectly fine without it.

1 TABLESPOON CORN OIL
1 LARGE ONION, FINELY CHOPPED
500 ml CHICKEN OR VEGETABLE STOCK
3 POTATOES, DICED
500 g CLAMS, CHOPPED
3 TABLESPOONS YOGHURT
1 TABLESPOON PARSLEY
1 TEASPOON TAMARI OR SOYA SAUCE
PINCH CAYENNE PEPPER
PAPRIKA, TO GARNISH

Heat oil and gently sauté onion until soft. Gradually add stock and, when boiling, add potatoes. Simmer till tender – this takes 15-20 minutes, depending on the size of the potatoes. Add clams and cook a further 5 minutes. Stir in yoghurt, chopped parsley, tamari and cayenne and allow to heat through but do not boil. Sprinkle with paprika and serve hot.

PUMPKIN SOUP

1 TABLESPOON BUTTER
1 ONION, CHOPPED
2 CLOVES GARLIC, CRUSHED
PINCH NUTMEG
GOOD PINCH CINNAMON
PINCH CUMIN
PINCH VEGISALT
PINCH CHILLI POWDER
1 SMALL PUMPKIN, PEELED AND CHOPPED
500 ml CHICKEN OR VEGETABLE STOCK
250 ml MILK
PAPRIKA, TO GARNISH

Melt butter and gently sauté onion and garlic for 5 minutes. Sprinkle in nutmeg, cinnamon, cumin, vegisalt and chilli powder and continue to cook until onions are tender. Add pumpkin and stock and cook 20 minutes or until vegetables are soft. Purée in a food processor or blender or push through a sieve. Return to heat and stir in milk. Heat through but do not allow to boil, garnish with paprika and serve hot.

SHRIMP MOUSSE

This is known here as Prawn Mousse!

500 g RAW PRAWNS, DEVEINED
125 ml CHICKEN OR VEGETABLE STOCK
4 TABLESPOONS WHITE WINE
1 TABLESPOON GELATINE
3 TABLESPOONS COLD WATER
1 SMALL ONION, FINELY CHOPPED
1 TEASPOON TARRAGON
1 TABLESPOON TOMATO PURÉE
1 TABLESPOON LEMON JUICE
PINCH VEGISALT
PINCH CAYENNE PEPPER
125 ml WHIPPED CREAM

Place raw prawns in boiling sock and white wine for 3-4 minutes or until they are pink. Remove prawns and allow to cool. Meanwhile, soften gelatine in cold water for 5 minutes, then stir into the stock until it dissolves. Allow to cool. Chop prawns and mix together with onion and tarragon. This can be done either by hand or in a blender or food processor until smooth. Add tomato purée, lemon juice, vegisalt and cayenne, then fold in whipped cream. Pour into a wet mould and chill for 2 hours. Unmould by running a small, sharp knife around the edge of the mousse, then dip the mould quickly into a bath of hot water. Place a chilled plate on top of the mould, invert and then tap once or twice. The mousse will slide out gently. Garnish with a little extra mayonnaise and fresh herbs such as tarragon, watercress or dill.

SHRIMP FILLED PEPPERS

4 FIRM RED OR GREEN CAPSICUMS
2 TABLESPOONS OLIVE OIL
1 LARGE ONION, FINELY CHOPPED
2 CLOVES GARLIC, CRUSHED
500 g PRAWNS
1 CUP COOKED BROWN RICE
1 TABLESPOON PARSLEY
1 TABLESPOON CHIVES
1 TEASPOON TAMARI
PINCH CAYENNE PEPPER
1 EGG, LIGHTLY BEATEN
3 TABLESPOONS BRAN
2 TABLESPOONS BUTTER

Plunge capsicums into boiling water for 3 minutes and then into cold water. This firms the capsicums. Remove from cold water, cool and then halve from top to bottom. Remove seeds and chop finely. Add capsicum insides to heated olive oil and sauté gently. Stir in onion, garlic, prawns, rice, parsley, chives, tamari and cayenne and cook over a low heat for 10 minutes, stirring often. Stir in egg and cook 5 minutes longer. Stuff capsicums and lay in buttered baking pan. Sprinkle with bran, dot with butter and bake for 20 minutes in a hot (400°F/200°C) oven.

AMERICAN WILD RICE

2 TABLESPOONS BUTTER
1 CARROT, DICED
1 STICK CELERY, CHOPPED
1 SMALL ONION, CHOPPED
500 g WILD RICE (OR LONG GRAIN BROWN RICE)
500 ml CHICKEN OR VEGETABLE STOCK
250 g MUSHROOMS, SLICED
1 CUP PEAS, FRESH OR FROZEN

Melt 1 tablespoon butter and gently cook carrot, celery and onion until soft. Add rice, stir well, then pour in stock. Cover and cook 40-45 minutes or until all the stock is absorbed and the rice is done. Meanwhile, melt remaining tablespoon of butter and cook sliced mushrooms gently. Cook peas and drain. Add cooked peas and mushrooms to rice and serve hot.

JAMBALAYA

1 TABLESPOON OIL

3 RASHERS BACON (OPTIONAL)

1 ONION, CHOPPED

2 CLOVES GARLIC, CRUSHED

1 GREEN CAPSICUM, CHOPPED

500g RAW BROWN RICE

375ml CHICKEN OR VEGETABLE STOCK

500g TOMATOES, SKINNED AND CHOPPED

1 TABLESPOON MINCED CELERY

1 BAY LEAF

500g PRAWNS OR OYSTERS

FRESHLY GROUND BLACK PEPPER

PINCH CAYENNE PEPPER

1 SPRIG THYME

PINCH VEGISALT

PARSLEY TO GARNISH

Sauté bacon (or heat 1 tablespoon oil) then add onion and garlic. Cook till soft, then add capsicum and brown rice. Cook for a couple of minutes stirring constantly, then gradually add all remaining ingredients except parsley. Simmer gently 40 minutes or until rice is done and most of the moisture is evaporated. Garnish with parsley.

VEGETARIAN CHILLI

Chilli is a favourite dish of the South West although it is usually made 'con carne' – with meat. Traditionally served with Three Bean Salad, this Vegetarian Chilli is a delicious alternative.

1 CUP TOMATO JUICE

1 CUP CRACKED WHEAT

2 TABLESPOONS OLIVE OIL

2 ONIONS, CHOPPED

3 CLOVES GARLIC, CRUSHED

2 STICKS CELERY, CHOPPED

2 CARROTS, CHOPPED

1 GREEN CAPSICUM, CHOPPED

1 TEASPOON BASIL

1 TEASPOON APPLE CIDER VINEGAR

PINCH CHILLI POWDER

1 TEASPOON TAMARI

2 TABLESPOONS TOMATO PASTE

3 TABLESPOONS DRY RED WINE (OPTIONAL)

4 TOMATOES, PEELED AND CHOPPED

500g COOKED RED KIDNEY BEANS

PARMESAN CHEESE

CHOPPED PARSLEY

Bring tomato juice to boil and pour over cracked wheat. Leave to swell while you prepare the vegetables. Heat oil and sauté the onion and garlic till soft. Add celery, carrots and capsicum and cook for 5-10 minutes, then stir in basil and vinegar. Add a good pinch of chilli powder and cook a few minutes over a low heat. Add tamari, tomato paste, wine and tomatoes, cover and simmer gently for 25-30 minutes or until all the flavours are combined. Serve with hot kidney beans, freshly ground Parmesan cheese and chopped parsley.

CELERY VICTOR

This recipe originated in San Francisco, although it can now be found in salad bars all over the country.

3 BUNCHES CELERY

250 ml CHICKEN OR VEGETABLE STOCK

A FEW SPRIGS FRESH PARSLEY

1 BAY LEAF

A FEW PEPPERCORNS

6 TABLESPOONS OLIVE OIL

3 TABLESPOONS WHITE WINE VINEGAR

PINCH VEGISALT

FRESHLY GROUND BLACK PEPPER, TO TASTE

Garnish

12 ANCHOVIES *OR* 6 SLICES TOMATO

12 STRIPS PIMENTO

6 SLICES HARD-BOILED EGG

EXTRA PARSLEY

Cut the tops off the celery, leaving the hearts — these are about 6 inches/150 mm long. Trim and clean them well, halve and place in a pan. Cover with stock, parsley, bay leaf and peppercorns and simmer gently for 15 minutes. When cooked, remove celery hearts to serving dish. Mix together oil, vinegar, vegisalt and pepper and pour over celery while still warm. Allow to cool then refrigerate for 1 hour. Serve garnished with criss-crossed anchovy fillets and pimento strips or egg, tomato and a little soya mayonnaise. Garnish plate with extra parsley.

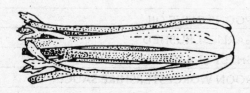

FOURTH OF JULY POTATO SALAD

4 POTATOES, COOKED AND DICED

1 AVOCADO, CHOPPED

5-6 SHALLOTS, CHOPPED

3 TABLESPOONS MUNG BEAN SPROUTS

1 TEASPOON CAPERS

2 EGGS, HARD BOILED

1 SMALL ONION, FINELY CHOPPED

2 STICKS CELERY, FINELY CHOPPED

1 TABLESPOON PARSLEY, CHOPPED

Dressing

3 TABLESPOONS SOYA MAYONNAISE

PINCH VEGISALT

1 CLOVE GARLIC, CRUSHED

1 TEASPOON APPLE CIDER VINEGAR

Place salad ingredients in a large bowl. Place dressing ingredients in a glass jar. Screw the lid on tightly and shake vigorously. Pour dressing over salad and toss lightly.

CAESAR SALAD

This Californian speciality is served in many areas of the United States.

1 LARGE COS LETTUCE, TORN INTO BITE SIZED PIECES

3 SLICES WHOLEMEAL BREAD, DICED

6 TABLESPOONS OIL

Dressing

6 TABLESPOONS OLIVE OIL

1 CLOVE GARLIC, CRUSHED

1 EGG, LIGHTLY BEATEN

1 TABLESPOON WORCESTERSHIRE SAUCE

3 TABLESPOONS LEMON JUICE

SALT AND PEPPER, TO TASTE

Garnish

8 ANCHOVIES

500 ml PRAWNS (OPTIONAL)

FRESHLY GRATED PARMESAN CHEESE

3 TABLESPOONS WALNUTS (OPTIONAL)

Wash the lettuce, dry and chill so that it is crisp. Fry the diced bread in the hot oil, drain on paper towels and allow to cool. These croutons should also be very crisp and crunchy. Whisk all dressing ingredients together, either by hand or in a blender or food processor and pour over the lettuce leaves. Garnish with croutons, parsley and Parmesan and, if using, prawns and walnuts.

MUFFINS

Easy to make, easy to eat. All sorts of things can be added to muffins, from fruit such a bananas, apples, strawberries and peaches to dried fruit, dates, coconut, spices, cheese and nuts.

2 CUPS WHOLEMEAL FLOUR, SIFTED

1 TEASPOON VEGISALT

2½ TEASPOONS BAKING POWDER

2 EGGS

3 TABLESPOONS OIL

1 CUP MILK

1 TABLESPOON HONEY

½-1 CUP FRUIT, NUTS OR SPICES

Mix together flour, salt and baking powder. Combine eggs, oil, milk and honey in a separate bowl, then pour into dry ingredients. Mix well, add fruit, nuts or spices and fill greased muffin (patty) tins. Bake at 400°F/200°C for 20-25 ıminutes or until the muffins are firm.

GRIDDLE CAKES

These are the traditional American pancakes, generally served with butter and maple syrup or cream and fruit.

250g WHOLEMEAL FLOUR, SIFTED

2 TEASPOONS BAKING POWDER

1 TEASPOON VEGISALT

3 EGGS

375ml MILK

4 TABLESPOONS OIL

2 TABLESPOONS HONEY

Combine flour, baking powder and vegisalt. Mix together eggs, milk, 2 tablespoons oil and honey. Pour wet ingredients into dry ingredients and stir well. Leave batter to rest for at least 30 minutes. To cook, heat oil and swirl mixture thinly onto a very hot griddle or frying pan. Cook for 2 minutes then flip over with a spatula and cook the other side for a further 2 minutes. Stack pancakes onto a heated plate and keep warm until ready to serve.

CAROB BROWNIES

125g BUTTER

3 TABLESPOONS HONEY

3 TABLESPOON MAPLE SYRUP

2 EGGS

1 TEASPOON VANILLA ESSENCE

125g WHOLEMEAL FLOUR, SIFTED

125g CAROB POWDER

1 TEASPOON BAKING POWDER

125g WALNUTS, CHOPPED

Cream butter, honey and maple syrup. Stir in lightly beaten eggs and vanilla then add remaining ingredients. Pour into buttered baking tin (a shallow tin such as a lamington tin would be best) and bake in a moderate (350°F/180°C) oven for 30 minutes. Allow to cool, then cut into squares.

ALLIGATOR PEAR, FLORIDA STYLE

The 'alligator pear' is actually an avocado!

3 RIPE AVOCADOES

1 LEMON, JUICED

3-4 TABLESPOONS HONEY

WHIPPED CREAM OR YOGHURT

Mash the avocadoes, add lemon juice and sweeten with honey. Beat till smooth and stir in a little whipped cream or yoghurt. Pile into serving dish and serve chilled with cream or yoghurt and extra honey or maple syrup.

AMERICAN APPLE PIE

The definitive American dish...

2 PIE CRUSTS (SEE PECAN PIE RECIPE)

4-6 APPLES, PEELED AND SLICED

3-6 TABLESPOONS HONEY, DEPENDING ON TARTNESS OF APPLES

2 TABLESPOONS ARROWROOT *OR*

1 TABLESPOON FLOUR

1 TABLESPOON LEMON JUICE

¼ TEASPOON NUTMEG

½ TEASPOON CINNAMON

Roll out one of the pie crusts and line a buttered and floured pie dish. Fill the pie with apples, heaping them high around the centre. The pie will look very full, but the apples do shrink. Now mix together the honey, arrowroot or flour, lemon juice and spices. Pour this mixture over the apples. Cover the pie with the remaining crust. Crimp the edges and use the extra pastry to decorate the top of the pie with leaves. Brush with melted butter or lightly beaten egg white. Cut a couple of small gashes in the pastry to allow steam to escape then bake in a hot oven (450°F/220°C) for 10 minutes. Reduce heat to 350°F/180°C and bake for a further 25-30 minutes or until the pastry is golden brown and perfect.

SOUTHERN PECAN PIE

1 UNBAKED PIE CRUST (SEE FOLLOWING RECIPE)

4 EGGS

1 CUP CORN SYRUP OR MAPLE SYRUP

125 g BUTTER, MELTED

1 TEASPOON VANILLA ESSENCE

½ CUP HONEY

1 TABLESPOON WHOLEMEAL FLOUR

200 g PECAN NUTS, CHOPPED

Beat eggs lightly then stir in remaining ingredients. Fill pie crust with pecan mixture and bake for 40-45 minutes in a moderate (350°F/180°C) oven. Serve warm or cooled with whipped cream or sweetened yoghurt.

UNBAKED PIE CRUST

4 TABLESPOONS BUTTER

1 CUP WHOLEMEAL FLOUR, SIFTED

1 TABLESPOON MAPLE SYRUP

¼ CUP ICED WATER

The secret of a good pie crust is to chill all the ingredients and to handle the pastry as little as possible. Cut butter into the sifted flour then drizzle maple syrup over this mixture. Work with finger-tips until mixture resembles breadcrumbs, then gradually add iced water until a dough is formed. Refrigerate dough for 30 minutes then roll out gently on a lightly floured board. Try to do this as quickly as possible. Lift pie crust onto a buttered pie dish. push down gently and prick base with a fork. Neaten edges by cutting with a knife, then fill pie as required.

THE CARIBBEAN

There's nothing like a little Caribbean soul to bring some sunshine into a cold winter's day. In a part of the world where summer never fades, tropical fruits and vegetables combine with exotic seafoods in an unusual way. It is sometimes said that there is no really distinct Caribbean cuisine and certainly there are noticeable influences from other parts of the world. Spanish, French, Indian and Chinese cooking – some of the more palatable relics of past imperialism – all offer their best aspects in the food of the Caribbean islands.

The end result is unique, for the delicious, spicy fare of the West Indies today is aflame with colour and soul and – with a little imagination – the tastes of the fruity, tropical dishes resonate with the buzz of cicadas on balmy nights and the excitement of the islands at Carnivale time...

MELON MUSTIQUE

2 MEDIUM SIZED CANTELOUPES OR MELONS

3 TABLESPOONS SOYA MAYONNAISE

1 TABLESPOON TOMATO PUREE

DASH CHILLI SAUCE OR A PINCH OF CHILLI POWDER, TO TASTE

SALT AND PEPPER, TO TASTE

200g PRAWNS, COOKED AND PEELED

100g ROASTED PEANUTS, SKINNED

2 LIMES OR 1 LEMON, CUT INTO WEDGES

Halve the melons, scoop out the seeds and cut out the flesh with a melon baller or with a dessertspoon. Smooth out the melon shells and then put in the fridge to chill. Mix together mayonnaise, tomato paste, chilli, salt and pepper. Add the melon balls – or dice the melon if it is in chunks – prawns and peanuts to the mayonnaise mixture. Pile into the melon shells and serve cold, garnished with chives and lime or lemon wedges.

PLANTAIN CHIPS – *Tostones de Platanos*

Green banana delicacies that can be enjoyed either hot or cold. The plantain looks exactly like a green banana but it is a vegetable rather than a fruit and must be cooked. You will find plantains for sale at good fruit shops. This recipe also works quite well using green bananas if you have trouble finding plantains.

2 RIPE PLANTAINS

3 TABLESPOONS WHOLEMEAL FLOUR

2 TEASPOONS CINNAMON

3 TABLESPOONS OIL

Cut the plantains into chips. Mix together the flour and cinnamon and toss in the plantain chips until they are evenly coated. You may need a little more flour, depending on the size of the plantains. Heat the oil and fry the coated plantains quickly until golden on all sides. Drain and serve hot or cold.

SEA SOUL DIP – *Mojor de Pesces*

A spicy fish dip.

125g RICOTTA CHEESE
30g CREAM CHEESE
2 TABLESPOONS FRESH LIME OR LEMON JUICE
200g COOKED WHITE FISH, MINCED
SEA SALT AND CAYENNE PEPPER, TO TASTE
1 TABLESPOON PARSLEY, FINELY CHOPPED
1 TEASPOON DILL, FINELY CHOPPED
1 TABLESPOON MILK
PINCH PAPRIKA, FOR GARNISH
EXTRA CHIVES, FOR GARNISH

Beat the ricotta and cream cheese together with the lime or lemon juice. Work in the minced fish and blend till smooth. Add salt and cayenne to taste then blend in parsley, chives and dill. Thin to required consistency with milk and then pile into a bowl. Sprinkle with paprika and garnish with chives. The consistency of this dip can be modified by altering the amount of milk used.

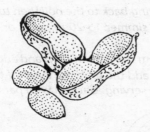

CALYPSO CHOWDER – *Sopa de Camarones*

A meal in itself.

30g BUTTER
1 LARGE ONION, FINELY CHOPPED
2-3 CLOVES GARLIC, CRUSHED
750g TOMATOES, SKINNED AND CHOPPED
250ml VEGETABLE OR FISH STOCK
1 BAYLEAF
PINCH CLOVES
SALT AND PEPPER, TO TASTE
CHILLI POWDER, TO TASTE
2 LARGE POTATOES, SCRUBBED CLEAN AND CUT INTO QUARTERS
3 COBS FRESH CORN
250g PRAWNS, COOKED AND PEELED
PARSLEY, FOR GARNISH

Melt butter and sauté onion and garlic till soft. Add tomatoes, stock, bayleaf, cloves, salt, pepper and chilli powder. Bring slowly to the boil, stirring constantly, then reduce heat and leave to simmer for 15 minutes. Purée in a blender or through a sieve and then return to the pot. Bring back to the boil then toss in the scrubbed potatoes, reduce to simmer 15-20 minutes or until potatoes are cooked.

Scrape kernels from the cobs of corn and add to the soup. Simmer 5 minutes then add the prawns. Turn off the heat and leave for 5 minutes before serving. Garnish with parsley and enjoy!

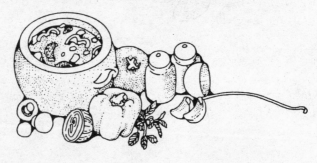

TRADE WIND SOUP

A warming peanut soup to take the chill from the air when the Trade Winds blow

60 g BUTTER
60 g WHOLEMEAL FLOUR
1½ LITRES VEGETABLE OR CHICKEN STOCK
375 g CRUNCHY PEANUT BUTTER
PINCH CAYENNE PEPPER
PINCH NUTMEG
A LITTLE CHOPPED PARSLEY, FOR GARNISH

Melt the butter and stir in flour to form a roux (a little ball which comes away from the sides of the pot). Cook for 2 minutes, stirring all the while then gradually add 1 litre (2 pints) of the stock. Bring to the boil then reduce to simmer. In a separate bowl, blend the remaining stock with the peanut butter and then add this to the hot soup. Season to taste with cayenne pepper and nutmeg and simmer 10 minutes longer. Garnish with a little chopped parsley.

SWEET POTATO FRITTERS

Nice with a crunchy green salad or with the chicken or fish dishes which follow.

2 LARGE SWEET POTATOES
2 EGGS, LIGHTLY BEATEN
75 g BUTTER
SEA SALT AND FRESHLY GROUND BLACK PEPPER, TO TASTE
½ CUP WHEATGERM
4 TABLESPOONS OIL

Wash and peel the sweet potatoes. Cut into small pieces and cover with cold water. Bring to boil and cook till tender. Drain and mash then stir in eggs, butter, salt and pepper. Allow to cool then form into patties. Coat with flour first, then the extra egg, then wheatgerm. Chill till firm then fry in oil till golden brown.

JAMAICAN CARROTS

1 COCONUT, SPLIT IN HALF TOGETHER WITH RESERVED COCONUT MILK

500g CARROTS, GRATED

2 CRISP APPLES, FINELY SLICED

2 TABLESPOONS OIL

1 TABLESPOON CIDER VINEGAR

1 TABLESPOON CURRY PASTE, HOT OR MILD ACCORDING TO TASTE

SALT AND PEPPER, TO TASTE

1 TABLESPOON RAISINS

1 TABLESPOON PINE NUTS

1 SMALL, CRISP LETTUCE

Set aside a little coconut for decoration then coarsely grate the rest. Mix the grated coconut with carrots and apples. Place the strained coconut milk, oil, vinegar, curry paste, salt and pepper into a clean glass jar. Screw the lid on tightly and shake vigorously. Pour dressing over coconut, carrot and apple mixture then stir in raisins and pine nuts. Arrange on a bed of lettuce and garnish with a few strips of coconut. These look very effective if carved finely with a potato peeler.

BAKED YAM AND ORANGE

2 LARGE OR 3 MEDIUM SWEET POTATOES

5 LARGE ORANGES

4 TABLESPOONS YOGHURT

2 TABLESPOONS BUTTER

SALT AND PEPPER, TO TASTE

2 TABLESPOONS PARSLEY, FINELY CHOPPED

Wash and peel the sweet potatoes then cook in boiling water till tender. Drain and mash. Slice the tops off four of the oranges and scoop out the flesh, making sure you keep the shells intact. Cut the tops into thin strips and save for decoration. Grate the rind of the fifth orange and squeeze the juice from it. Add yoghurt, butter, salt and pepper to the cooked sweet potatoes. Beat in the grated orange rind and enough orange juice to make the mixture moist but not sloppy.

Spoon the potato mixture into the orange shells and bake at 350°F (Gas 4) for 20 minutes or until brown on top. Garnish with orange strips and chopped parsley.

CRUNCHY CUKES

An unusual way of serving cucumber as a hot, cooked vegetable rather than as a salad ingredient.

4 SMALL CUCUMBERS

SALT

4 RASHERS BACON (OPTIONAL)

1 EGG, BEATEN

1 CUP (125 g) BRAN

125 g BUTTER

1 TABLESPOON CHIVES, CHOPPED

Slice cucumbers and place in a colander, sprinkling liberally with salt. Set aside for 30 minutes to drain. Remove rind from bacon, cut into pieces and fry slowly until crisp. Remove from pan and keep warm. Remove cucumbers from colander and pat dry with a clean tea towel or kitchen paper then toss in egg and breadcrumbs. Heat butter in the same pan the bacon was cooked in and fry the cucumbers until golden. Toss in the bacon and stir gently. Remove to serving plate and garnish with chives.

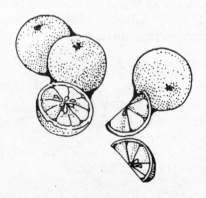

CARIBBEAN KEBABS

Delicious cooked on a barbecue or grill, Caribbean Kebabs taste of the sun.

Marinade

30 g BUTTER

1 LARGE ONION, CHOPPED

2 CLOVES GARLIC, CRUSHED

2 TABLESPOON TAMARI OR SOYA SAUCE

PINCH CAYENNE PEPPER

2 TABLESPOONS CURRY POWDER

2 TABLESPOONS HONEY

2 TABLESPOONS CIDER VINEGAR

Heat the butter and sauté onion and garlic till soft. Add tamari, cayenne, curry powder, honey and vinegar and put into a large, shallow bowl.

Kebabs

750 g PRAWNS, SCALLOPS OR FIRM WHITE FISH

2 FIRM BANANAS OR PLANTAINS

2 MANGOES, CUT INTO CUBES

1 PAWPAW, CUT INTO CUBES

1 SMALL PINEAPPLE, CUT INTO CUBES

Place the prawns, scallops and/or fish in the marinade for several hours or overnight. When ready to use, drain the seafood and thread onto skewers alternately with the banana, mango, pawpaw and pineapple cubes. Warm the marinade while cooking the kebabs over a hot grill or barbecue plate. Pour the marinade over the kebabs and serve with plain rice.

TRINIDAD PRAWNS

Another pretty, festive dish – this time filling pineapple halves with curried prawns.

2 TABLESPOONS OLIVE OIL

1 LARGE ONION, FINELY CHOPPED

3 CLOVES GARLIC, CRUSHED

2 TABLESPOONS SHREDDED COCONUT

2 TABLESPOONS BLACK MUSTARD SEEDS

PINCH CAYENNE PEPPER

1 TABLESPOON CURRY PASTE – OR ALTERNATIVELY MORE OR LESS, ACCORDING TO TASTE

2 TOMATOES, SKINNED AND CHOPPED

2 TABLESPOONS COCONUT CREAM

2 kg PRAWNS, COOKED AND PEELED

2 MEDIUM SIZED PINEAPPLES

Heat the oil and sauté the onion and garlic for 5 minutes. Add shredded coconut, mustard seeds, cayenne, curry paste and cover to cook over a low light for a further 10 minutes, stirring from time to time to prevent catching. Add tomatoes, coconut cream and prawns, stir and cover. Leave to simmer slowly for a further 10 minutes. Meanwhile, halve the pineapples lengthways, scoop out the flesh and fill with the prawn mixture. Decorate with pieces of fresh pineapple and serve with rice.

CHICKEN IN COCONUT SHELLS – *Pollo con Coco*

Pretty and festive, this dish calls for coconut halves. It is easy to halve a coconut if you pierce the little holes at one end of the coconut and drain out the milk, which you should always reserve as it is a wonderful nectar. Place the coconut on a hard surface with the holes facing downwards and tap sharply with a hammer. In this way, you should get a good, clean break.

2 LARGE, RIPE COCONUTS, BROKEN INTO HALVES

30 g WHOLEMEAL FLOUR

SALT AND PEPPER, TO TASTE

PINCH CAYENNE PEPPER

PINCH POWDERED GINGER

PINCH POWDERED CLOVES

2 TEASPOON POWDERED THYME

1 kg COOKED CHICKEN, DICED

100 g BUTTER

3 TABLESPOONS RUM

125 ml SOUR CREAM

1 SMALL CANTELOUPE, DICED OR SCOOPED INTO BALLS

Scoop the coconut flesh out of the shell, remove any hard brown skin and grate. Toast the grated coconut in a heavy bottomed pan until golden, shaking all the time to prevent burning. Reserve to use later. Combine the flour, salt, pepper, cayenne, ginger, cloves, thyme and coat the chicken in this mixture. Melt the butter and fry the coated chicken for 5 minutes or until brown. Add the rum and sour cream and keep warm but do not allow to boil. Divide the mixture evenly between coconut halves, garnishing each with melon balls and toasted coconut. Serve immediately.

CREOLE COD – *Bacalao Criollo*

If you can't get cod, any tasty white fish will do.

3 TABLESPOONS OLIVE OIL

1 LARGE ONION, FINELY CHOPPED

1 CLOVE GARLIC, CRUSHED

1 LARGE CAPSICUM, GREEN OR RED, FINELY CHOPPED

2 TABLESPOONS FLOUR

SALT AND PEPPER, TO TASTE

1 TEASPOON LEMON RIND, FINELY GRATED

PINCH CHILLI POWDER – OR FRESH CHILLIS TO TASTE

500 g FRESH COD, SKINNED AND CUT INTO PIECES

250 g SMALL PRAWNS, COOKED AND PEELED

500 g TOMATOES, SKINNED AND CHOPPED

250 ml YOGHURT

PAPRIKA, TO GARNISH

Heat oil and sauté onion, garlic and capsicum for 5 minutes. Blend in flour, salt and pepper and stir well.

Add lemon rind, chilli, cod, prawns and tomatoes, stirring gently. Cover, reduce heat and leave to simmer for 20 minutes. Stir in yoghurt and remove to serving dish. Garnish with paprika and serve at once.

PLANTER'S PUNCH – *Ron Santa*

Rum is the spirit of the sugar cane and the spirit of Jamaica. It would be impossible not to include a recipe for at least a couple of rum drinks for hundreds of varieties are concocted throughout the Caribbean.

3 TABLESPOONS (75 ml) DARK RUM

1 TABLESPOON (25 ml) ORANGE JUICE

1 TABLESPOON CASTER SUGAR OR HONEY

A DASH OF ANGOSTURA BITTERS

Shake the above ingredients together in a cocktail shaker or mix in a blender or food processor. Pour over ice and serve with a straw.

DAIQUIRI

Internationally famous, the Daiquiri originally came from the Virgin Islands.

1 TABLESPOON (25 ml) ORANGE JUICE

1 BANANA, MASHED

3 TABLESPOONS (75 ml) DARK RUM

Blend orange juice and banana in a processor or beat with a whisk until frothy. Add rum and pour over ice.

BARBADOS BANANAS

The sweetness of the bananas contrasts with the sharpness of lime juice, the mellowness of rum and the tang of spices in this extravagant, flaming dessert.

4 FIRM, RIPE BANANAS

2 TEASPOONS LIME JUICE – OR LEMON JUICE IF LIMES AREN'T AVAILABLE

30 g BUTTER

250 ml RUM

125 g DARK BROWN SUGAR

PINCH NUTMEG

PINCH CINNAMON

PINCH GINGER

1 TABLESPOON FRESHLY GRATED ORANGE RIND

2 TABLESPOONS PEANUTS, SKINNED AND FINELY CHOPPED

Peel and slice the bananas into quarters. Sprinkle with lime juice. Heat the butter and brown the bananas lightly. Mix together the rum, reserving 1 tablespoon for later use, sugar, nutmeg, cinnamon, ginger and orange rind. Place the bananas in a buttered, oven-proof dish and pour over the rum mixture. Top with chopped peanuts and bake at 350°F (Gas 4) for 15 minutes. Remove from oven then, just as you are about to serve, put the reserved rum in a ladle, set alight then pour over the bananas. Serve flaming with whipped cream or honey-sweetened yoghurt.

JAMAICAN GINGER BREAD

The molasses in this ginger bread makes it irresistibly rich, dark, moist and delicious.

3 CUPS WHOLEMEAL FLOUR

2 TEASPOONS POWDERED GINGER

1 TABLESPOON FRESHLY GRATED ORANGE RIND

4 TABLESPOONS SOFT BROWN SUGAR

125g BUTTER

250g MOLASSES

½ TEASPOON BICARBONATE OF SODA

4 TABLESPOONS WARM MILK

2 EGGS, BEATEN

Mix together flour, ginger and orange rind. Melt sugar, butter and molasses over a low light until the sugar completely dissolves. Dissolve the bicarbonate of soda in the milk then beat in the eggs. Alternately add the sugar mixture and the egg mixture to the flour mixture, beating well. Pour into a buttered and floured square cake tin and bake at 300°F (Gas 2) for 1¾ hours. Turn out onto a rack to cool. This ginger bread keeps well in an air-tight tin.

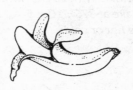

PAPAYA FLAN

*The ubiquitous flan or caramel custard appears here in a most
unusual form.*

1 LARGE RIPE PAWPAW, PEELED AND SEEDED

3 TABLESPOONS COCONUT CREAM

125 ml CREAM

125 ml MILK

½ TEASPOON VANILLA ESSENCE

3 EGGS, SEPARATED

PINCH GINGER

60 g BROWN SUGAR

1 TEASPOON FRESHLY GRATED ORANGE RIND

PINCH NUTMEG

*Blend pawpaw in a food processor or blender or pass through a
sieve — this should produce about 2-3 cups purée. Combine with
coconut cream then spread in the bottom of a buttered oven-
proof dish. Warm the cream, milk and vanilla but do not boil.
Beat the egg white till fluffy. Beat the yolks together with the
ginger, sugar and orange rind until smooth. Add the egg yolk mixture to the cream and milk then fold in the egg whites. Pile on top
of pawpaw mixture, sprinkle with a little nutmeg then place dish
in a pan of hot water. Bake at 375°F (Gas 5) for 30 minutes or until
the custard is set. Serve hot or cold.*

CARIB CAROB CAKE

Delicious accompanied by a cool mango or mint sorbet, this carob treat is included here on highly suspect grounds, getting in simply by the semantic skin of its very sweet teeth!

250 g PLAIN WHOLEMEAL BISCUITS

125 g CAROB, IN BLOCK FORM

2 TABLESPOONS HONEY

60 g BUTTER

1 TEASPOON RUM

½ TEASPOON VANILLA ESSENCE

60 g WALNUTS, CHOPPED

HALF AN ORANGE

Crush the biscuits between two sheets of greaseproof paper with a rolling pin to make fine crumbs. Break up the carob and melt over a low light with honey, butter, rum and vanilla. Remove from heat and stir in biscuit crumbs and walnuts until the mixture clings together in a mass. Spread into an oiled sandwich tin, smoothing off the top with half a cut orange. Mark off slices with a knife and put in the fridge to set. When cold and firm, turn out onto foil. Break into slices, wrap and return to fridge until required.

MANGO ICE

1 RIPE MANGO

500 ml SOUR CREAM

3 TABLESPOONS HONEY

Peel mango and mash with a fork or blend in food processor till smooth. Stir in sour cream and honey and beat till creamy. Pour into ice tray and cover. Freeze till half frozen and remove. Beat again with a wooden spoon or in a food processor then return to freezer until firm.

MEXICO

Fiesta in Mexico means dancing, fireworks and processions.
It also means 'feast' – and feasting in Mexico means enjoying a
great variety of national and regional dishes that have developed
out of indigenous Aztec, Spanish, Arabic and even French
cuisines.

Many people mistakenly assume that all Mexican food is hot
and fiery and laced with an over-abundance of chillis. Admittedly,
there are a lot of hot dishes, but there are also subtle ones, such
as Huachinango a la Veracruzano (Red Snapper with sweet yellow
capsicum and capers), Tamales de Oaxaca (chicken and cornmeal
steamed in banana leaves) and the famous Mole Poblano (turkey
in a spicy sauce containing nuts and chocolate... yes, chocolate!).

Mexican food in Mexico doesn't seem to have all that
much in common with the 'Mexican' food in other countries. The
recipes which appear below are traditional, regional ones rather
than the better-known, popularised versions of dishes such as
Chile con Carne or Tacos.

MEXICAN SOUP – *Sopa Mexicana*

Traditionally made with pork, I prefer a lighter, vegetarian version of this lovely green and golden soup.

1 TABLESPOON OLIVE OIL

3 MEDIUM-SIZED COBS OF CORN

3 MEDIUM-SIZED ZUCCHINI

4 LARGE TOMATOES

2 LITRES VEGETABLE STOCK

SEA SALT AND FRESHLY GROUND BLACK PEPPER, TO TASTE

50g CREAM CHEESE

2 AVOCADOS, PEELED AND SLICED

Heat the oil in a heavy-based saucepan, then add the corn, zucchini and tomatoes. Cook over a moderate flame for 5 minutes, stirring well. Gradually add the stock and reduce flame. Leave to simmer for 30 minutes. Season with salt and pepper. Add cheese cut into small squares and avocado slices just before serving.

AVOCADO PATÉ – *Guacamole*

Tiny pieces of crisp bacon, grated cheese, tomato, olives, chopped hard-boiled egg or cucumber can all be added to give an extra dimension to this delicious paté.

3 MEDIUM-SIZED AVOCADOS

2 CLOVES GARLIC, CRUSHED

1 LEMON, JUICED

1 ONION, FINELY CHOPPED

2 SMALL CHILLIES, FINELY CHOPPED

SALT AND PEPPER, TO TASTE

Mash the avocados thoroughly and then mix in the remaining ingredients. It is best to use the guacamole *soon after preparing, to prevent it turning brown.*

THE SAUCES OF MEXICO

Sauces have always been part of the Mexican tradition. The Aztecs called the sauce mole, and hence we have guacamole, the well-known avocado sauce which is used to accompany fish, vegetables or corn chips, or served simply as a salad on a bed of lettuce. The following recipes for Hot Chilli, Nachos and Yucatan Sauces are all equally versatile... and they are the key to good Mexican food.

HOT CHILLI SAUCE

2 TABLESPOONS OLIVE OIL

1 ONION, CHOPPED

2 CLOVES GARLIC, CRUSHED

PINCH GROUND CORIANDER

PINCH VEGISALT

PINCH FRESHLY GROUND BLACK PEPPER

1-2 SMALL CHILLIS, FINELY CHOPPED (OR ½ TEASPOON CHILLI POWDER)

4 TOMATOES, SKINNED AND CHOPPED

¼ TABLESPOONS TOMATO PASTE

125 ml WATER

1 TABLESPOON DRY RED WINE

Heat oil and sauté onions and garlic for 5 minutes. Add coriander, salt, pepper and chilli, stirring well. Cook for a further 5 minutes before adding tomatoes, tomato paste, water and wine. Leave to simmer 30 to 45 minutes, or longer. The longer you cook it the 'hotter' it will be. You can, of course, vary this by adding more or less chilli.

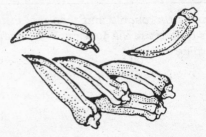

NACHOS SAUCE – *Salsa de Nachos*

You can use the Mexican beer-cheese sauce to accompany refritos, rice, tortillas or corn chips.

2 CUPS HOT CHILLI SAUCE

1 LARGE GREEN CAPSICUM, FINELY CHOPPED

500 ml BEER

1 TEASPOON BLACK SUGAR OR HONEY

250 g GRATED CHEESE

Warm the hot chilli sauce gently. Add the capsicum and beer, stirring frequently for about 20 minutes. Leave to simmer over a very low light for 1 hour, stirring occasionally to prevent sticking. Remove from heat, add sugar, and leave to stand for an hour or so. When you wish to use the sauce, reheat it gently, adding the cheese. Serve piping hot.

YUCATAN OLIVE SAUCE – *Salsa Yucateco*

Specially good with baked fish, this unusual olive sauce also teams well with rice, salad, or empanadas.

2 LARGE ONIONS, FINELY CHOPPED

3 CLOVES GARLIC, CRUSHED

3 TABLESPOONS OLIVE OIL

2 CAPSICUMS, CHOPPED

1 TABLESPOON SWEET PAPRIKA

1 LARGE ORANGE, JUICED

75 g GREEN OLIVES, PITTED

1 LEMON, JUICED

1 TEASPOON GROUND CORIANDER

SALT AND BLACK PEPPER, TO TASTE

Sauté onions and garlic in oil for 5 minutes. Add remaining ingredients and simmer for a further 10 minutes.

TORTILLAS

Tortillas *form the basis of many Mexican dishes. They are flat circles of bread made from a type of cornmeal called* masa harina, *not always commercially available. You can substitute wholemeal flour or experiment, using a combination of flour and cornmeal.*

500g WHOLEMEAL FOUR
PINCH SEA SALT
1 TABLESPOON BUTTER
250ml COLD WATER

Sift together flour and salt. Cut in butter, then add enough water to form a stiff dough. Knead on a lightly-floured surface, then divide into 10 balls. Roll each one as thinly as possible, then fry in a lightly-greased, heavy pan for about 3 to 4 minutes on each side.

CHEESE TORTILLAS – *Quesadillas*

500g WHOLEMEAL FLOUR
1 TEASPOON BAKING POWDER
100g CREAM CHEESE
4 TABLESPOONS BUTTER
1 EGG

Sift flour and baking powder. Mix in cheese, butter and egg, then leave to stand for 15 minutes. Divide into about 20 sections and roll each quesadilla *into a thin circle. Place a tablespoon of the following filling on each one, fold over and fry quickly until golden brown on both sides.*

Filling

1 CUP CHICKEN, COOKED AND DICED
1 TOMATO, SKINNED AND CHOPPED
1 ONION, FINELY CHOPPED
SALT AND PEPPER, TO TASTE
1 TABLESPOON OLIVE OIL

Cook all ingredients in oil over a moderate flame.

VEGETABLES

Even though many of the world's vegetables such as corn, beans, tomatoes, capsicums and avocados originally came from Mexico, Mexicans themselves are not fond of 'plain vegies'. Instead, they dress them up and serve them in elaborate sauces, stuffed with meat, formed into soufflés, pies, patties or casseroles, and garnished with brightly coloured pomegranate seeds or vivid orange squash flowers.

ZUCCHINI IN WALNUT SAUCE – *Calabacitas en Nogada*

Chillis, squash, chicken and veal can also be served en nogada, *that is, in a subtly spiced sauce of finely chopped walnuts dotted with bright pink pomegranate seeds.*

6 LARGE ZUCCHINI

½ SMALL CAULIFLOWER

2 ONIONS, FINELY SLICED

2 TABLESPOONS OLIVE OIL

3 CLOVES GARLIC, CRUSHED

100 g PINE NUTS

100 g RAISINS

1 TEASPOON LEMON PEEL

1 TABLESPOON VINEGAR

SALT AND PEPPER, TO TASTE

1 LARGE AVOCADO, DICED

PINCH CINNAMON

1 POMEGRANATE

SPRIG PARSLEY

Steam zucchini until tender, then cut in halves lengthwise and scoop out the centres. Steam cauliflower and chop roughly. Heat oil, then gently fry the cauliflower for 3 minutes or so. Add the garlic, stirring well, then add pine nuts, onions, raisins and lemon peel. Cook for a few minutes before adding vinegar, salt, pepper, avocado, cinnamon and pomegranate seeds. Fill the zucchini shells with this mixture, cover with nut sauce and garnish with parsley.

NUT SAUCE – *Salsa Nogada*
(for use in the recipe above)

100g WALNUTS, FINELY CHOPPED

6 TABLESPOONS BREADCRUMBS

1 TABLESPOON VINEGAR

50g ALMONDS, FINELY CHOPPED

50ml (¼ CUP) WATER

1 TABLESPOON BLACK SUGAR

1 POMEGRANATE (OPTIONAL)

Combine all ingredients thoroughly and garnish with pomegranate seeds.

SPINACH TIMBALES – *Timbalitos de Espinaca*

1 LARGE BUNCH SPINACH OR SILVER BEET, COOKED AND FINELY CHOPPED

2 TABLESPOONS BUTTER

2 TABLESPOONS CREAM

2 EGGS, LIGHTLY BEATEN

1 SMALL ONION, FINELY CHOPPED

SEA SALT AND FRESHLY GROUND BLACK PEPPER, TO TASTE

6 STRIPS BACON (OPTIONAL)

2 HARD-BOILED EGGS

Combine spinach with softened butter, cream, eggs, onion, salt and pepper. Butter 6 individual moulds and divide mixture between them. Press in firmly and place in a pan of hot water. Bake in a moderate 180°C (350°F) oven for 20 minutes. Turn moulds out onto a warmed platter and garnish with slices of crisp bacon and hard-boiled egg.

PUMPKIN MUFFINS – *Molletes de Calabaza*

You can substitute honey for the vegisalt and drizzle honey or maple syrup over these muffins to convert them from a savoury to a sweet.

1 CUP PUMPKIN, COOKED AND MASHED

150 ml (¾ CUP) MILK

1 BEATEN EGG

200 g (1½ CUPS) WHOLEMEAL FLOUR

1 TEASPOON VEGISALT

3 TEASPOONS BAKING POWDER

Mix together pumpkin, milk and egg. Add sifted flour, salt and baking powder. Pour into muffin (deep, round, individual) tins and bake at 220°C (425°F) for 30 minutes.

MEXICAN RICE – *Arroz Mexicana*

1 CUP LONG GRAIN RICE

1 TABLESPOON OLIVE OIL

½ TEASPOON CUMIN

1 SMALL RED CAPSICUM

1 CLOVE GARLIC, CRUSHED

1 SMALL ONION, FINELY CHOPPED

1 LARGE TOMATO, CHOPPED

SALT AND PEPPER, TO TASTE

500 ml (2½ CUPS) CHICKEN OR VEGETABLE STOCK

1 TABLESPOON CHOPPED PARSLEY

1 TABLESPOON CHOPPED GREEN OLIVES

Soak rice for 30 minutes in cold water. Drain and leave to dry for 1 hour. Brown rice in heated oil, then add cumin, finely chopped capsicum, garlic, onion, tomato and seasoning. Add stock gradually. Cover and cook for 25 minutes or until all the liquid has been absorbed and the rice is soft. Garnish with parsley and olives.

MEXICAN BEAN SALAD – *Ensalada de Frijoles*

200 g KIDNEY BEANS, COOKED

100 g PEAS, COOKED

1 SMALL LETTUCE, SHREDDED

200 g BUTTER BEANS, COOKED

1 LARGE ONION, FINELY SLICED

200 g SALAMI (OPTIONAL)

Combine all ingredients and toss gently in the following dressing.

4 TABLESPOONS OLIVE OIL

1 TABLESPOON LEMON JUICE

SALT AND PEPPER, TO TASTE

1 TABLESPOON TOMATO PASTE

1 TABLESPOON WHITE WINE VINEGAR

2 CLOVES GARLIC, CRUSHED

¼ TEASPOON CHILLI POWDER

Place all ingredients in a glass jar. Screw the top on tightly and shake well. Drizzle over salad.

VERACRUZ RED SNAPPER – *Huachinango à la Veracruzano*

In Mexico, seafood is almost synonymous with the historical port city of Veracruz. Huachinango à la Veracruzano *is one of the rare Mexican dishes that contains absolutely no chilli!*

125 ml (6 TABLESPOONS) OLIVE OIL
1 SMALL ONION, FINELY CHOPPED
1 SWEET YELLOW PEPPER, DICED
2 TOMATOES, FINELY CHOPPED
½ TEASPOON BLACK SUGAR
½ TEASPOON LEMON JUICE
1 TABLESPOON CAPERS
50 g GREEN OLIVES, PITTED AND CHOPPED – RESERVE A FEW WHOLE OLIVES FOR GARNISH
500 g RED SNAPPER FILLETS
3 SLICES BREAD
1 TABLESPOON CHOPPED PARSLEY

Preheat the griller so that it is very hot. Heat 2 tablespoons of the oil in a frying pan and gently cook the onion until it is transluscent. Add the sweet yellow pepper (you can substitute a sweet red capsicum if you prefer), cook for a few minutes, before adding tomatoes, sugar, lemon juice, capers and olives. Cover and leave to simmer. Meanwhile, brush the fish with oil and grill quickly – about 5 minutes a side. Place in a serving dish and cover with the sauce. Place under the still-warm griller. Cut bread into triangles and fry in the rest of the oil until golden. Remove fish from griller and garnish with fried bread, olives and parsley. Serve with steamed or boiled potatoes and a green salad.

TURKEY IN PUEBLA SAUCE – *Mole Poblano*

Mole poblano is virtually a national institution in Mexico and is found on the table of every fiesta – from christenings and marriages to funerals. You can substitute chicken for turkey to make mole sencillo, or 'simple mole' if you prefer.

3 GREEN CAPSICUMS, FINELY CHOPPED

2 SMALL, HOT CHILLIS, CHOPPED

2 TABLESPOONS SESAME SEEDS

30g COOKING CHOCOLATE, UNSWEETENED

PINCH ANISEED

½ TORTILLA

1½kg TURKEY (OR CHICKEN), STEWED GENTLY AND CUT INTO SERVING PIECES

2 RED CAPSICUMS, FINELY CHOPPED

2 TABLESPOONS OLIVE OIL

2 TABLESPOONS CHOPPED PEANUTS

1 SMALL STICK CINNAMON

SEA SALT, TO TASTE

100 ml (½ CUP) WATER

Soak the capsicums and chillis in water for 30 minutes. Drain and then cook in the heated oil. Add the sesame seeds, peanuts, chocolate, aniseed, cinnamon, salt and fried tortilla and stir well. Add the water, cover and continue to cook over a low light for 5 minutes or until the sauce thickens. Cover the hot turkey (or chicken) with the mole sauce and simmer for about 10 minutes. Serve very hot with plain, steamed rice.

DESSERT

Mexican cuisine is not renowned for its fabulous desserts. They are mostly ultra-sweet, syrupy concoctions and so I have only included one here – but this is a very good one. It is flan supremo, not the traditional, national dessert which has evolved from the French creme caramel, but a delectable chestnut custard which is uniquely Mexican.

SUPREME CUSTARD – *Flan Supremo*

500g CHESTNUTS (OR 1 CAN CHESTNUT PUREE)

500ml MILK, SCALDED

3 LIGHTLY BEATEN EGGS

1 TEASPOON VANILLA ESSENCE

30g (1 TABLESPOON) HONEY

PINCH NUTMEG

Cut a cross in the top of each chestnut and bake in a hot 260°C (500°F) oven for 15 minutes. Remove shells and skins, boil for 20 minutes, drain and then purée in a blender, food processor or through a sieve. Mix in milk, honey, eggs and vanilla and beat well. Pour into a buttered baking dish, sprinkle with nutmeg and place in a pan of hot water. Bake slowly 150°C (300°F) for 1 hour or until set. Remove from water and allow to chill before serving. NOTE If using canned and sweetened chestnut purée, omit honey.

INDEX